DEVELOPING RESEARCH PROPOSALS

SUCCESS IN RESEARCH

The Success in Research series has been designed by Pam Denicolo and Cindy Becker to provide short, authoritative and accessible guides for students, researchers and academics on the key area of professional and research development.

Each book is written with an eye to avoiding jargon and each aims to cut to the chase of what readers really need to know about a given topic. These are practical and supportive books and will be essential reading for any students or researchers interested in developing their skills and broadening their professional and methodological knowledge in an academic context.

SUCCESS IN RESEARCH

DEVELOPING RESEARCH PROPOSALS

PAM DENICOLO · LUCINDA BECKER

Sage

Reprint 2023

Originally published in 2012

This South Asia edition published in 2012

Sage

Sage Publications India Pvt Ltd
Unit No. 323-333, Third Floor, F-Block
International Trade Tower
Nehru Place
New Delhi - 110 019, India

Exclusively Distributed in South Asia by

ATLANTIC
PUBLISHERS & DISTRIBUTORS

7/22, Ansari Road, Darya Ganj, New Delhi
Tel.: +91-11-4077 5252, 2327 3880
E-mail: orders@atlanticbooks.com
Web: www.atlanticbooks.com

Published by Sonia Kumar for Sage Publications India Pvt Ltd.

ISBN: 978-81-321-1023-1 (PB)

This book is dedicated to all the research students who have taught us so much as their supervisors or in our Graduate School roles, and to all the colleagues with whom we have shared struggles, disappointment and elation when seeking research funding to pursue our various intellectual passions.

CONTENTS

LIST OF BOXES, ACTIVITIES, TABLES AND FIGURE

Boxes

Activities

Tables

Figure

ABOUT THE AUTHORS

Professor Pam Denicolo, a chartered constructivist psychologist, has a research commitment to improving learning and teaching in H.E., focusing on the needs of graduate students, their supervisors and other professionals seeking to develop their practice. Her passion for supporting graduate students and other early career researchers is demonstrated through her numerous successful doctoral candidates and her lead roles in national and international organisations such as the UK Council for Graduate Education, the International Study Association on Teachers and Teaching, the Society for Research into Higher Education Postgraduate Network, the Impact and Evaluation Group and other working groups of Vitae, and the QAA Doctoral Characteristics Advisory Group, all of which have resulted in many publications, presentations and workshops.

Dr Lucinda Becker, an award-winning Senior Lecturer and Teaching Fellow in the Department of English Language and Literature at the University of Reading, has spent her career committed to enhancing the skills of undergraduates and research postgraduates. She has written numerous successful study skills guides for students. As a professional trainer she also works throughout the United Kingdom and Europe, devising and delivering training in communication and management techniques, principally to lawyers, engineers and scientists.

Pam and Cindy worked exuberantly together for many years managing and developing the Graduate School at the University of Reading and providing a substantial contribution to its research methods, generic skills and doctoral supervisor training.

PROLOGUE

SERENDIPITY

The world of research – and particularly of successful research proposals – is replete with examples of serendipity. There is a conundrum in your discipline area that has been puzzling you for some time, niggling away at the back of your mind; you spot information on a website about opportunities to study for a doctorate that indicates that proposals are being sought in the general intellectual realm of your previous studies; it is brought home to you by a particular personal circumstance that this might be a good time to engage in further study – the possibility of applying to study for a PhD becomes enticing. Or instead, perhaps you notice some potential connections between objects or ideas; a chance arises to talk your notions through with a colleague who agrees that the possibilities look intriguing; over coffee you notice in a professional publication that your discipline funding body has a call-out for bids to do research on a topic that fits in with your new ideas – the scene is set for you to begin writing a research proposal for funding.

Recently serendipity paid us a visit: a publisher (SAGE) emailed to ask about the potential for a book on proposal writing – the mail went to the foot of the large pile of things to think about; the next day students in our Graduate School requested a workshop on how to get further funding once they had completed their studies. Later that week a colleague from Student Recruitment met one of us at a meeting and bemoaned the parlous state of applications she had received, requiring her to request more polished proposals before she could pass them on to potential supervisors. The heap of tasks 'yet to do' had not decreased but the combined signals made us retrieve the publisher's mail. Perhaps there was something worth following up but was there really enough to say to fill a book?

We sent out messages to colleagues across a range of disciplines to solicit key points they would want to include in guidance to proposal writers. Their very useful responses indicated that there are concerns in common related to the quality of proposals and the need for some down-to-earth guidance. The sub-topics they noted were each worthy of chapters in their own right: when a proposal is needed, where to find funding, how to write **aims** and **objectives**, what should be included in the methods section, how much detail is needed in the budgeting section, where you can get support ... this book began to quietly gestate while we considered its range of coverage and who might be its readership. (Note that terms in bold are defined in the Glossary.)

INTENDED READERS

We decided that we should not lose sight of those who originally inspired the book – early career researchers either seeking to begin doctoral research or to move on from that first large stepping stone into the world of funded research. Thus this book may prove helpful to you if you aspire to register for a research degree or if you are in the first few years of a paid career in research and keen to (or simply must) acquire funding to continue your research. We recognise that people come to both of these life points having had a range of prior experience and having developed a variety of skills and, equally, needing to polish up or even acquire others. Therefore we have provided guidance on each of the many facets of research proposals, moving rapidly from a basic level to the much more sophisticated level required for success.

We intend this book to serve those of you embarking on the preparation of a research proposal for the very first time, leading you carefully through the whole process. Obviously some, perhaps many, of you will have already had experience in writing proposals but have not had the success you would like. You will find that you can move more rapidly through the text seeking points that are new to you or that are presented in a way to stimulate a new approach to your writing. However, we recommend that you do at least skim through the areas that you may already have some expertise in because you may find in them that little bit of spice that will help you tickle the taste buds of your future reviewers.

Moreover, throughout this book we will engage in discussion related to proposals both to support applications for *research degree* places and to solicit *research funding*. We judged that while good proposals in each realm have their own peculiarities, there is enough common ground to provide general advice and caveats for both. As with disciplinary differences or variations in research requirements in different countries, we note distinctions between them as we tell the main story. So in general much of what we say will relate to both kinds of proposal but whenever we want to make specific points about either we will italicise those relevant words early in the paragraph to help you navigate the text and focus on your specific interest. However, again we would recommend you read all chapters through quickly to start with to build up your general understanding of the what, why and wherefore of proposal preparation and writing. You can then return to chapters that need a bit more of your attention, perhaps to engage in the activities we suggest there to develop your skills. If you have never produced a proposal before you should find that completing all of the activities leaves you with material that will contribute to a proposal which will only need some coordination and a little refinement before submission.

OVERVIEW OF THE BOOK

Chapter 1 provides an overview of the whole process of producing a proposal, with attention paid to the different situations you might inhabit as a researcher and the different skills and purposes you bring to the task. It particularly emphasises the importance of getting to know your audience and how to organise the effective preparation of your proposal so that each task can be accomplished in a timely manner. Chapter 2 provides more detail about the specific purposes of different kinds of proposals, those for gaining a place, and perhaps financial support for, a research degree (master's or doctoral degrees that have a significant research component) and those for obtaining funding for a specific research project. It includes an overview of the sections required in most if not all proposals and why they are important to those who will review your proposal and those who will make final decisions about it.

Later chapters introduce you to the wider preparation needed to embark on writing the proposal. For instance, in Chapter 3 the importance of layout, tone and style is discussed, particularly as it relates to different funding bodies, while Chapter 4 urges you to consider the theoretical perspective taken and the required extent of the **literature review**. It offers a range of practical advice about engagement with the literature and how you might present it in relevant sections of the proposal. Chapter 5 involves a detailed discussion and demonstration of that really important aspect of the proposal, the **research questions** or hypotheses, including which of these is the more appropriate for your proposed field of enquiry. Chapter 6 focuses on research methodology, beginning with justifying the general philosophical approach and theoretical framework, then describing the **design** and implementation of a research plan and rounding off with the data analysis techniques envisioned, each with a rationale for their choice. Financial matters, which can never be avoided, form the substance of Chapter 7, which includes a review of funding sources as well as guidelines for preparing a budget.

The remaining chapters concentrate on timing and **research organisation** issues, on other people involved in the process and on responding to results, reflections and anticipations. Chapter 8 provides guidance on how to present the organisation of your research in a plan, noting the timeline and milestones for the research project, which will convince reviewers that you can accomplish it on time. The following chapter (Chapter 9) reviews the importance of referees and other potential contributors, how to choose them and make best use of their support. It also provides information about the review process so that you can orientate your proposal accordingly. Finally, Chapter 10 considers responses to success and rejection, reviews the main learning points, elaborates on final preparation and submission guidelines, and reflects on the value of proposal writing for your future career.

Each chapter includes several practical activities that should contribute to your proposal development, as well as several reflection points so that you can review your own progress in thinking about and working on your proposal.

THE TASK BEFORE YOU

After this overview you must be thinking that proposal preparation is a lot of hard work. To be successful, it is. Each proposal needs to be a cogent, detailed argument that will convince reviewers that you have the expertise, energy and commitment for them to take the risk of investing scarce resources to support you. There are a lot of stakeholders involved with any piece of research. For instance, the careful preparation of your proposal is the first part of your investment in your research career. Those of you contemplating signing up to do a research degree will be considering the impact of it on your time and resources (and on family, friends and perhaps work colleagues); think too about the commitment required of your chosen institution and of your supervisors/advisors, tutors and support staff. Similarly, research funders owe a responsibility to those who provide their finance (including you, as a taxpayer) to ensure that their money is spent wisely. If they spend it on your research then some other research project is rejected.

So you can see that you have to be fussy, like all the other stakeholders, to at least stand a chance in this competitive environment. Do not contemplate wasting your time, and that of those involved in the first sift review of your proposal, by giving in to the temptation of using one of the many 'cheat sites' for preparing proposals that can be found on the web. Not only are reviewers sophisticated enough to spot a pro forma version of a research proposal, but also, as you will see as you work through the chapters that follow, a common theme is that each different organisation has very specific, idiosyncratic requirements to which they will expect successful applications to adhere. You will be required to weave an understanding of their needs and context into a demonstration of your personal expertise that should make you stand out in a crowd.

If you still, after this preamble, want to become a successful researcher, then the only way forward is to take a deep breath and commit to investing the many weeks, and often months, required to prepare a polished and convincing proposal. This will provide a solid foundation for your degree or funded project in the future so it is just as important to convince yourself that it describes a viable and valuable research endeavour as it is to capture the attention and support of external reviewers. You must also be pragmatic and consider the possibility that no matter how cogent your proposal, it may not succeed, at least at first. Proposal writing is part of the routine life of an academic. Having a proposal accepted is less common but is thus more gratifying than other standard pursuits. So we will endeavour to be realistic in this book, introducing you to both the highs and the lows of proposal writing, approaches to embrace and to reject, caveats to consider and encouragements to relish.

We wish you luck and fortitude and invite you to start with Chapter 1. May you enjoy the journey as well as the destination!

1

WHAT IS A RESEARCH PROPOSAL?

CHAPTER OVERVIEW

This chapter discusses:

- the nature of research proposals;
- the general range of skills required to develop proposals;
- disciplinary and national differences in requirements;
- the first steps in meeting the needs of your readership, whether seeking a research degree place or funding for research or both.

A PERVASIVE TASK DEFINED

For those wishing to engage in research, as a career in itself or as part of an academic engagement, there is no escape from the rigours of writing research proposals. Whether you are at the beginning of your research career, contemplating applying for a university place to study for a research degree, or whether you are a new contract researcher or academic seeking funding to begin or continue your research work, you will be faced with the task of writing a research proposal in an extremely competitive environment. Before you begin, let us first summarise the task, as a prelude to exploring it in depth. A research proposal, in whatever context, is intended to convince others that you have a relevant and interesting topic to research that will provide (in some explicit way) useful results and a sensible idea of how to set about that research in a timely, economical way. In other words, you must convince your target audience that the research itself is worthwhile and that you are an ideal, competent person to conduct it.

A range of skills and expertise is needed for the task of proposal writing as well as for the research that follows a successful application. Therefore this book is intended to help those who are unfamiliar with the process of proposal writing or who want to improve their chances of success in a complex and demanding field. Indeed, some of the skills and abilities required can be transferred directly from other pursuits once their relevance and importance is understood; others may exist but need some re-alignment to fit the context and yet others may need to be learned. The UK Researcher Development Statement, and its detailed listing of descriptors of attributes across the phases of academic development – the Researcher Development Framework (RDF) (Vitae, 2010) – provide an indication of the diversity of accomplishment and proficiency required at each stage of a research career. Many of these skills and attributes relate directly or indirectly to the writing of research proposals. This should reassure you that you probably have some of the skills required of proposal writing already; you simply need some guidance on when and how to apply them.

We will return to the RDF later (as part of an activity) because we intend to provide a guide to help you identify those attributes that you already possess, those that need some polishing or modification and those that you will be best advised to acquire. In this particular chapter we will start the process by unpicking what the general purpose of a research proposal is from the perspectives of those who require you to present one, so that you can become familiar not just with what you need to achieve in writing the proposal, but why you need to include the various components. Details of the priority of each component, depending on context, will emerge throughout the book.

A CELEBRATION OF DIFFERENCE

We are conscious that each reader will be in different circumstances, those particularly pertinent to this task of research proposal writing being:

- living and working in diverse parts of the world, perhaps even contemplating a location move;
- links to a particular discipline or small group of disciplines;
- full- or part-time degree registration and/or level of paid employment;
- working/studying within or at a distance from a Higher Education institution (HEI);
- varied extent and recency of prior experience of study;
- current range of relevant skills and attributes.

To begin with the last on the list, in order to emphasise that you do have skills that you can bring to the task, and to help you map your progress in developing other relevant skills, we provide you at the end of this chapter with an activity that will allow you now and in the future to chart some relevant attributes. Your chart will be specific to you and will enable you to judge which of the suggested further reading materials provided are most relevant for you and which areas of the proposal might need extra attention and perhaps greater peer review (supportive criticism from colleagues – see Chapter 9) before submission.

Although the general focus of this book will be on generic information about the task, and advice relevant to a range of disciplines, we will draw your attention to disciplinary differences where appropriate. Between us, the authors, we have worked in disciplines in the arts and humanities, the social and the natural and life sciences and we have made good use here of our contacts across the disciplines to provide examples and references that highlight any subtleties or distinct differences in purpose, approach and requirements for proposals between disciplines or discipline areas.

Each country will, of course, have its own research funding providers, each of whom will have some degree of idiosyncrasy in its requirements, while universities within any one country, never mind between countries, will have specific entry requirements and interest in different aspects of a limited range of research topics. In this book we will mainly follow the requirements of UK funders and Higher Education institutions (HEIs), but we will note any differences from other locations that we are aware of and will provide some references to books and articles from other countries that might prove useful to you. However, although the main propositions, advice and caveats are universal, with differences appearing mainly in required formats or particular detail (information about which is usually supplied by the funder or HEI to applicants), it will save you time and heartache to heed our advice that follows about how to tailor your proposal to suit each specific institution or funding organisation.

You may have some good ideas already, and even perhaps a first draft of a proposal prepared, but it is nonetheless crucial that you obtain as much information as is available from the particular funding body (or for each funding body) or academic provider that you intend to approach. They are as individually different as each of you as readers are. Draft outlines, or particular paragraphs about detail, may well be transferable between applications but each funder/HEI will have particular style and format requirements as well as requiring some pieces of information that others may not. For instance, the restrictions on word length can vary substantially while protocols for section headings and content also differ. We urge you to resist any urge to produce a generic application to be sent out to any and every funder or university you know; instead, gather your ideas, hone them into good shape but customise them to fit the requirements of each specific audience. Meticulous attention to the guidance notes of the relevant organisation will pay dividends and save heartache. Some relevant websites can be found in Appendix 1. In that appendix we have included some suggestions that attend to the diversity of background and circumstance that you bring with you to the task.

FIRST STEPS IN MEETING THE NEEDS OF YOUR READERSHIP

All recipients will need to be reassured about certain things, which we will address further in Chapter 2, but you will also need to capture their attention early in the proposal form and keep them reading because they will receive a myriad of proposals containing good research ideas from competent people. The world of research is a very competitive environment so one purpose of a proposal is to convince those who have a restricted number of places for research degrees and/or limited financial resources to allocate that your research deserves some special attention. There is some mutuality in this in that your audience too wants to recognise in your proposal that their organisation is receiving some special attention from you – after all you are formulating a proposition that you will work closely with and for them in the future. No one will look fondly at a proposal from an uninterested suitor! So we urge you to start your proposal effort with a little preliminary research about your target readership.

FINDING OUT ABOUT RESEARCH DEGREE OPPORTUNITIES

In most instances documents related to *research degrees* can be found on institutional websites so you will be able to explore the particular emphases in each institution you are interested in. (This initial interest may be because of location, previous experience of yourself or family/friend, or because of its general reputation, etc. Keep in mind that you may need to spread your net more widely to find the best match with your own needs, attributes and ambitions.) You will see that all are seeking to ensure that every student they accept on a programme of study has a very good chance of success in their study environment; this is in their interest because they want to avoid wasting their time, energy and resources. For instance, they will be seeking students who can provide evidence of having a range of what we might call academic skills, for instance, evidence contained in a curriculum vitae that demonstrates appropriate previous study and experience as well as an application that is written with an appropriately sophisticated attention to style, grammar and spelling. After all, a key aspect of research is dissemination which requires the development of many forms of communication to a high level. We will follow this up in Chapter 3, which will include suggestions for people applying for study using a language that is not the one they most frequently use.

Various combinations of academic qualifications and work experience are deemed acceptable to most HEIs but the exact balance will depend on discipline and the culture of the institution. For instance, in some subject areas, particularly those with a strong professional link such as in education, law or the health professions, it is a positive advantage to have not only work experience but also a research project stimulated by issues arising in the professional context. In other subject areas, particularly in some rapidly developing science subjects, evidence of recent and relevant academic study in the focal area is essential. All will require a good standard of pass at first degree level, the rubric often referring to a first or upper second class degree or equivalent. The term 'equivalent' indicates that sometimes some professional qualifications or experience may be considered instead so it may be worthwhile, if you are in doubt about the perceived quality of your degree or do not have one, checking with the institution which other qualifications they will consider.

Some institutions have procedures for the accreditation of prior learning (APL) or for the accreditation of prior experience and learning (APEL). This may simply require you to furnish alternative certificates or may be a more demanding process, requiring the development of a portfolio of evidence to support your claims to relevant experience. Other institutions, or specific disciplines within an institution, may also require a master's level degree whilst yet others may accept a master's level qualification as compensating for a mediocre or non-existent first degree. There is some variation within and across HEIs and across HEI systems in different countries because each has different facilities and training/study programmes to bridge the gap between your present level of work and that required for a higher degree by research. Thus it is worth ensuring that you have selected appropriately before spending time on polishing up the rest of your proposal.

FINDING OUT ABOUT RESEARCH FUNDING OPPORTUNITIES

Proposals for *research funding* also require evidence of your academic mastery and prior experience of research to begin the process of judging whether you are a suitable candidate; that is, whether you are likely to have the knowledge and ability to undertake the research proposed. So it is important to check any requirements by funding bodies related to academic experience and success. For example, some HEIs will accept some students on research degrees with one level of academic qualification but require a much higher level from those for whom they are willing to provide their scarce scholarships or bursaries/studentships. Some funding bodies also have funds that are only available to very specific and restricted categories of people, such as particular professional groups (say health workers) or workers within particular organisations (say accredited institutions) or even those with certain personal attributes or backgrounds, depending on the source of the funding and any preference of the person/s providing it. So an extremely important first step in developing this kind of proposal is to check any such limitations in the sources of funding considered. This can usually be found under a heading such as: 'This resource/fund/bid is open to ...'.

In addition to ensuring that you do not fall at the first hurdle in the reviewing process, a careful examination of information about the organisation or institution will aid your task in other ways, whether you are seeking a place on a research degree or funding or both. Academic reviewers will certainly expect you to have done some exploration about them, what disciplines are taught, what research activity is currently a priority, and so on. Such preliminary research, which you should evidence in the way you write (see Chapter 3), indicates a commonsense approach, some embryonic skill at research and a genuine interest in the institution and those who work in it. They will expect you to be seeking to work in a compatible environment on a topic that is relevant to their current work and available expertise. A wise prospective student will also have familiarised themselves with the work and publications of their potential supervisors (or advisors, as they are called outside the UK) and target their proposal accordingly. You might include evidence of this by including in a covering letter or in your rationale section of the proposal an allusion such as: 'I note that in a recent article by Dr … that …'.

GENERAL PRELIMINARY EXPLORATIONS

Whether you are responding to a call for bids for funding or putting in a speculative proposal, having a knowledge of (and being able to demonstrate) the organisation's recent and relevant research interests similarly indicates efforts to be current in your understanding of and knowledge about the research topic in focus. A further benefit is that you can then target your proposal to fit into a developing area.

One of your first tasks, then, before you set finger to keyboard or pen to paper, is to do some preliminary research about your audience, the institutions or organisations who will be your proposal target and the people who will review your polished effort.

ACTIVITY 1 IDENTIFYING THE SKILLS REQUIRED OF A RESEARCHER

Find the website of (one of) the institutions or organisations who will be your proposal target audience. Download relevant documents and begin to prepare a profile description of the kind of researcher they are looking for by sifting through the material for clues. Include the qualifications required but also other important attributes that they seem to value.

For instance, is much made in the documents of the changing nature of the research context of the proposed subject so that 'flexibility' or 'versatility' might be valued? Do they require knowledge, achievements or skills beyond that of a specific subject, such as being able to speak another language, or converse with a wide range of people, or be able to travel away from base? Demonstrating survival skills when outside of our normal comfort zone may be very important in research that involves fieldwork, whereas the ability to use, or to demonstrate experience of prior use of, particular equipment and /or **instruments** may be valued for lab-based or studio-based research.

SKILLS INVENTORY

Another early task, one we referred to earlier, is to reassure yourself that you already have some of the skills required to prepare and write a proposal. To complement the activity above we have provided another activity based on ideas and simplified excerpts from the Researcher Development Framework (RDF) that we hope will motivate you to continue learning about the skills and processes involved and will guide you in deciding on which ones, and which parts of this book, need to be prioritised for attention. If you would like to explore the RDF further you can find both the full framework and a resource which is a simple Continuing Professional Development (CPD) tool for researchers, a downloadable Professional Development Planner, on the Vitae website: www.vitae.ac.uk/rdf

ACTIVITY 2 MAPPING SOME OF YOUR RELEVANT SKILLS

In Table 1 are a few of the descriptors in summary form that apply to researchers in general that we have selected to give you an insight into some of the attributes that reviewers will be looking for, or seeking evidence that you might soon achieve, in your proposal. Phase 1 describes research students with a good higher degree while Phase 2 would be more relevant to someone who has or is about to complete their doctoral studies or who is in the first years of employment as a professional researcher. Note that Phase 2 subsumes Phase 1 – it is a development from it. You should not expect to be able to tick all the boxes in Phase 1 if you are applying for a research degree place but you should be able to demonstrate potential for achieving most of them. Whatever your stage of development as a researcher there will be some qualities you may have to work on because none of us is perfect, but we have selected some that are particularly relevant to proposal writing.

Highlight those you feel describe you and note any evidence that you could provide to demonstrate this in the third column. The remaining ones provide you with areas on which you need to work, using this book, the further references listed or other resources.

The relevance of these descriptors will become more evident as you read the next chapter, which provides more detail about the purpose of a proposal from the point of view of those who receive it, describing the sections that you will find in most proposal forms, why they are included and the sorts of things you should therefore include.

TABLE 1 Researcher descriptors

Domain/ sub-domain	Descriptor phase 1	Descriptor phase 2	Potential evidence
Knowledge base/subject knowledge	Knows of recent advances within own research area and in related areas.	Is developing a knowledge of related and associated subject areas.	
Knowledge base/research methods	Understands and can apply relevant research methodologies and techniques and can justify their appropriate application within own research area.	Appreciates the value of, and can apply in appropriate contexts, a range of standards and methods/techniques for information/data collection and analysis.	
Knowledge base/ information seeking	Identifies and accesses appropriate bibliographical resources, archives and other sources of relevant information including web-based resources, primary sources and repositories.	Conducts advanced and complex searches using a range of sophisticated information software, resources and techniques; recognises their advantages and limitations.	
Knowledge base/academic literacy and numeracy	Writes clearly and in a style appropriate to purpose and context for specialist and non-specialist audiences.	Improves own style of texts for written or oral presentation.	
	Is mathematically competent to undertake research in own discipline/research area.	Understands any analytical or statistical procedures in related disciplines/ research areas and continues to develop mathematical ability.	
	Is IT literate and digitally competent, uses virtual networks for research.	Develops further necessary IT and digital skills.	
Cognitive abilities/ analysing and synthesising	Critically analyses and evaluates own findings and those of others. Validates datasets of others.	Has skilled and sharp analytical abilities, with knowledge of a range of methods.	
	Sees connections between sections of own information/ data and previous studies.	Critically synthesises new and complex information from diverse sources.	
		Has broad vision, recognises patterns and connections beyond own discipline/research area.	
Cognitive abilities/problem solving	Isolates basic themes of own research; formulates basic research questions and hypotheses.	Formulates and applies solutions to a range of research problems and effectively analyses and interprets research results.	
Cognitive abilities/ innovation	Understands the role of innovation and creativity in research.	Exercises critical judgement and thinking to create new and/or imaginative ways of understanding.	
	May engage in inter-disciplinary research.	Develops new ways of working on a topic and has unusual ideas.	
		Identifies which ideas are likely to be successful.	

REFLECTION POINT: REFLECTING ON YOUR CURRENT AND REQUIRED SKILLS AND ATTRIBUTES

You already have many of the skills and attributes required to write a successful research proposal but some will need to be re-orientated to the task, others will need to be polished and a few will need to be acquired. Reflect on which will fit into each category for you and decide on a plan to achieve an acceptable level for each.

2

WHEN IS A RESEARCH PROPOSAL REQUIRED AND WHY?

CHAPTER OVERVIEW

This chapter discusses:

- the issue of motivation and its influence on research choices;
- potential sources and mechanisms of financial support;
- information on funders' requirements;
- ways of selecting potential supervisory support;
- restrictions on scholarships;
- the purpose of a research proposal;
- general requirements of reviewers;
- the kinds of evidence to be included with a proposal.

MOTIVATION

From what we said in the previous chapter, and from your own motivation in selecting this book to read, it is clear that proposals are required when candidates are seeking either a place on a research degree programme or funding for research beyond a formal degree-awarding situation. Both of these involve the allocation of scarce resources so the competitive element is high. If you are seeking a degree place and funding for fees and maintenance then you can expect reviewers to be even more selective. Whether they are representing an HEI or an organisation that provides funding for research projects, reviewers will use the medium of the proposal to judge whether the investment, in terms of time, technical resources and money or a combination of those things, is not just worthwhile but is the best investment that can be made in the circumstances. They will be seeking evidence about the quality of the proposed research, your current knowledge and skills and indicators that you will remain motivated and engaged throughout the period of the research.

To convince others of your motivation you need to be clear yourself what is driving or inspiring you. For instance, you may be motivated to seek funding in order to:

- engage in research to add to a body of knowledge conceptually or empirically;
- address a theoretical or practical problem;
- translate theory or practice into a new arena;
- provide evidence to guide policy;
- improve practice;
- explore a previously unconsidered dimension of or perspective on theory/practice;
- combine some of the above aspirations.

All of these are laudable aims but each will appeal to different audiences. It is important that you seek the best match between your aims and abilities and the needs and requirements of those who might support you in any way. Therefore, before you firmly decide on the final audience for your proposal, it is important that you identify for yourself your own ambitions and why you want to achieve them before you start to try to convince others about your ability and suitability and the appropriateness of your research plans.

ACTIVITY 3 IDENTIFYING WHAT MOTIVATES YOU AND HENCE YOUR PROJECT CHOICE

Using the list above as a template, begin to identify which of those motivations are most important to you and try to articulate why that is so and why you might be a good, if not the best, person to do it. You should also give some thought to the nature of the research that you propose in terms of whether it requires a detailed pre-structured plan, with all aspects pre-determined, or whether the topic requires a more open-ended design, exploring an emerging field.

Such categories of research will appeal to different audiences so we will look next at why your audience might be interested in seeking or receiving proposals, and of what kind. Thus, it would be useful for you to have your ideas about what and why at least in draft summary, so that you can find a good match. We will explore how you propose conducting the research in Chapter 4.

SOURCES OF FUNDING

To be frank at the outset, it is far easier to get an offer for a place on a university research degree programme than to obtain research funding to support such studies or to support a research project when employed by a university or research institute. However, bear in mind that often you will have to secure an offer of a (usually specified) higher degree by research from an institution before applying. This is particularly so for 'internally funded' degrees, that is, funding from a source within the university in which you intend to pursue your study and research. Thus we have decided to tackle the most difficult aspect first in this chapter, returning to advice about how to begin seeking a place on a research degree course later.

Whatever your situation or plans, to obtain funding for research, either as a research student or as a member of staff, you should start work on your bids for financial support at least a year in advance of when you plan to start the research because, as we noted earlier, the competition is intense and you need to engage in a good deal of preparation before you can begin to write your proposals. This applies even to those of you who intend to respond to targeted calls for proposals on pre-selected themes, a topic we will discuss in more detail below. These usually require meeting very tight deadlines so having ready access to some pre-prepared materials that can be tailored to fit a range of potential bids is wise pre-planning. We have used the plural here expecting that you may have to try several avenues to stand a chance of success and you might need to consider adding together small amounts of funding in order to make up what you need. (Remember that if you hope to study full time for a *research degree*, you are likely to be seeking funding for course fees, for travel and maintenance and for research expenses such as equipment and conference attendance. More detail will be provided in Chapter 7 about creating a realistic budget for your enterprise.)

The first part of your preparation should consist of your identifying potential funders and then making yourself thoroughly familiar with all the requirements that apply to those proposals they may consider – for instance, in addition to any proposed host institution meeting the eligibility criteria, you yourself will need certain (excellent) qualifications and relevant experience to get on this first rung of the ladder, and then you need to make the most persuasive case possible. We cannot help you with obtaining the required qualifications but we can help you to build your case through these chapters. To get you started on this prior research to support your proposal writing, the avenues you should explore for funding a *research degree*, beyond your own and family resources, are:

- internal funding by the universities;
- research council funding;
- trusts and charities.

You might also be able to gain financial support or, simply but usefully, time for study such as day release from your own employer if you can make a good case that this activity would enhance your work and/or the work process generally.

For *funding for research projects* not connected to a research degree add to this list an exploration of commercial funders of research activity, including industrial sponsors.

We will supply a selection of relevant web contact details in Appendix 1 along with some references to literature which provide further sources. You should also explore which sources of funding are important in your field, such as those noted as sponsors at seminars, conferences and in research articles, and in addition consider finding out from colleagues in your research area which organisations have previously provided funding. You might also keep an eye on sources of funding alerts such as those found in *Research Fortnight,* an independent publication in the UK providing news about research.

ACTIVITY 4 RESEARCHING THE REQUIREMENTS OF RESEARCH FUNDERS

Once you have identified possible sources and set about finding out as much as possible about them, seek out answers to the following questions:

- What is the organisation's mission? What are their main interests and activities?
- What research topics have they funded recently? What do they say in their latest annual report on research? What approaches and methods do they seem to favour?
- What forms or application processes do they use (paper or electronic)? What rules do they have for submission, such as deadlines, length, degree of detail, specific sections?
- What criteria do they use to judge proposals (explicit and implicit)? What specific requirements do they have of researchers, especially in relation to eligibility, and what other specific conditions apply?

GAINING A RICHER VIEW OF FUNDERS' REQUIREMENTS

You can find up-to-date answers on the organisations' websites but you can get a fuller picture by contacting people who have recently received funding or even those who had a proposal rejected but with feedback. In addition to this, it is perfectly acceptable and often very helpful to make contact by writing or phoning, expressing your interest and asking sensible questions.

To give you a sense of the variation between funders, we provide here some information about UK sources and note in Appendix 1 some sources for European Union (EU) or overseas applicants as well as for those fulfilling home or residents' conditions.

There are seven research councils in the UK, each focussing on a particular group of disciplines, although increasingly they may link in various combinations to support multi- or inter-disciplinary research projects that fit their chosen prioritised themes within strategic frameworks. They are:

- Arts and Humanities Research Council (AHRC)
- Biotechnology and Biological Sciences Research Council (BBSRC)
- Engineering and Physical Sciences Research Council (EPSRC)
- Economic and Social Research Council (ESRC)
- Medical Research Council (MRC)
- Natural Environment Research Council (NERC)
- Science and Technology Facilities Council (STFC).

Those of you who have had some form of link with any of these research councils in the past may have heard of different forms of funding for various kinds of research, such as Directive Mode, Managed Calls and Directed Programmes (which referred to projects for which bids were sought within a particular time frame to investigate specified, high priority topics) or Responsive Mode projects (that were more open to the investigator to decide focus and date of submission of proposal). Similarly, although each council had slightly different procedures and requirements for prospective research students to follow to gain support for their research endeavours, by and large such students could expect to study at one of a large number of universities recognised as providing a good standard of research training. Following the Comprehensive Spending Review, in 2011 these research councils reviewed their own procedures for allocating their more limited resources, with the predominant outcome being that funding has become more focussed with a more restricted range of funding opportunities and a greater emphasis on strategic priorities that will have impact.

The following explanation was taken from the Research Councils UK website (www.rcuk.ac.uk) in February 2011:

Research Councils UK describe impact in the following ways:

ACADEMIC IMPACT

The demonstrable contribution that excellent research makes to academic advances, across and within disciplines, including significant advances in understanding, methods, theory and application.

When applying for Research Council funding via Je-S (see later), pathways towards academic impact are expected to be outlined in the Academic Beneficiaries section.

ECONOMIC AND SOCIETAL IMPACTS

The demonstrable contribution that excellent research makes to society and the economy. Economic and societal impacts embrace all the extremely diverse ways in which research-related knowledge and skills benefit individuals, organisations and nations by:

- Fostering global economic performance, and specifically the economic competitiveness of the United Kingdom
- Increasing the effectiveness of public services and policy
- Enhancing quality of life, health and creative output.

When applying for Research Council funding via Je-S, pathways towards economic and societal impacts are expected to be outlined in the Impact Summary and Pathways to Impact.

The reference to Je-S is to their electronic submission process while their website provides guidance on completing that section of the proposal named 'Pathways to Impact'. The strategic priorities of each research council can be found on their respective websites. Each funding source has strict criteria about who is eligible to apply, which will act as the first 'sift' in a complex process of proposal review. For research programmes funded by research councils in the UK, you must be a member of one of the institutions specified by them. Again we quote directly from the RCUK website:

> All UK Higher Education Institutions are eligible to receive funds for research, postgraduate training and associated activities. The higher education funding councils for England, Wales, Scotland and Northern Ireland determine whether an organisation meets the criteria to be a Higher Education Institute.
>
> Research institutes for which the Research Councils have established a long-term involvement as [a] major funder are also eligible to receive research funding, from any Council.
>
> Other independent research organisations (IROs) may also be eligible if they possess an existing in-house capacity to carry out research that materially extends and enhances the national research base and are able to demonstrate an independent capability to undertake and lead research programmes. They must also satisfy other criteria related to their financial and legal status: these are set out in full in the Research Councils' joint statement on eligibility.

We will discuss applying for a research council scholarship to undertake a research degree later in this section but it is clear that to maximise the possibility of gaining research council funding for research, your project must meet a more focussed set of criteria than previously, since funding will be concentrated in fewer institutions.

The number of charitable bodies funding research is also limited in number, some of the more famous being the Leverhulme Trust, which makes awards for the support of research and education; the Joseph Rowntree Foundation issues calls for proposals and invites submissions in response but 'does not accept speculative enquiries for funding'; and the Wellcome Trust, which is the world's largest medical research charity. Remember that a more comprehensive listing of bodies and useful websites is supplied in Appendix 1, which you should engage with as soon as you can to identify the potential resources that might fit your needs.

Given that comparatively few organisations provide funding in response to speculative bids, particularly at this time when research councils are having to focus their investment in research to achieve the very best value for an increasingly restricted amount of money, you might be more successful in achieving your aim of gaining *research funding* if you can orientate your particular research interest to fit comfortably within the framework of the current 'strategic challenges, priorities and impact objectives' of the relevant research council, the cross-council schemes and initiatives, or the current research focus of the charitable bodies. The relevant websites are a mine of information on these and on current projects with which yours might link. As you explore the websites do not neglect the FAQs for Applicants – these are the frequently asked questions that other people in your shoes have raised. As this chapter is being written, new information comes almost weekly from RCUK or one of the research councils so details are best sought directly when required, not neglecting the opportunity to telephone your preferred funding body directly with specific queries.

It is also important not to underestimate the value of talking your ideas through and sharing your draft proposals with others in your research area and adjoining ones because they can provide support, advice and perhaps even suggest useful collaborations to enhance your proposal. It is not just potential students who can benefit from the encouragement and assistance of experienced academics. In the next chapter we will mention their particular role during the writing process. For now, before seeking funders, consider making overtures and links with such colleagues while refining the focus of your research project.

GAINING FINANCIAL AWARDS FOR STUDY

Now we will look at the situation with regard to studentships and other awards for *higher degrees by research*. Universities in the UK vary greatly in whether they offer research studentships (including fees and a maintenance **grant** or stipend, as it may be known, at a rate that varies by institution, or simply fees only); research scholarships; or other forms of postgraduate funding such as from trust funds or legacies, most of which will have very specific conditions of eligibility. Funding may be available only for full-time study or may also be available for part-time enrolment, for home, EU, some specific nationalities or all overseas applicants. Fees may be funded fully or only partly. The ability to supplement income through research or teaching assistantship or demonstrator duties varies greatly and may be compulsory, available but optional or not available at all, throughout registration or only during particular phases of the research.

Research councils require prospective research students to apply through the registering university department, or through a research institute affiliated to a university, and have strict procedures and deadlines. They predominantly fund full-time study but are actively seeking ways in which collaborations with other funders might fund both full- and part-time study. Many have Case Awards, for instance (see the appropriate disciplinary council website) that they only partially fund but which can be topped up by collaboration with a public or government body. Most of the UK research councils now operate a system in which they allocate parcels of funding to cooperative units for research training which they judge provide exemplary research support and training. These are now much fewer in number than the previously 'recognised' units and are known variously, depending on the research council, as Doctoral Training Centres (DTCs), Centres for Doctoral Training (CDTs) or Doctoral Training Partnerships (DTPs), each of which may be combinations of departments across a single or multiple institutions. Others provide a block grant to selected research outlets which cover a range of disciplines in their remit. As we write, the move towards concentrating doctoral training scholarships within selected outlets is continuing so it will be worthwhile checking the latest news about which institutions are recognised outlets on the Research Councils' website (www.rcuk.ac.uk). In all of these cases, the research organisation will advertise the funding opportunities and hold a competition to select the students who will receive the scholarships, based on the quality of their proposals, their qualifications and other relevant attributes. It is worthwhile checking the requirements of both the research council and the doctoral training unit since the former may have given the latter a strong steer about what proportion of discipline topics to fund. There are some subjects/topics that are more strategic choices than others.

IDENTIFYING POTENTIAL SUPERVISORS/ADVISORS

Whether applying for university, research council or charity/trust funding, the support of a potential supervisor (known as an advisor in some countries) may be obligatory or voluntary but is always a bonus because such a person can guide you about relevance to the university and the funding body of a particular research project; can advise you about what approaches and methods can be appropriately supported by the institution and what training and resources are available; and can help orientate your project to meet the particular needs of the funding agency.

You should check the websites and/or prospectuses of universities that interest you, casting your net as wide as possible, to find details about such opportunities and also to identify the relevant academic staff with whom you might discuss your research ideas and ambitions. These sites are not all easy to navigate but you should look at the research interests and products, of academic staff in your discipline area (in other words, their completed projects and publications), and also consider the possibility of inter-disciplinary research which is increasingly in vogue. It may be easier to make contact initially with department or school directors of research or postgraduate research, or leaders (however titled) of Graduate Schools, who should be able to advise you about the availability of staff to support your project and perhaps give you contact details.

Do bear in mind that although the expert you require may appear on a staff list, this is no guarantee that they have space available on their research team. Also do not restrict your choice to the most eminent professor on the list; often a more junior colleague will have more time and availability to help you prepare your proposal and, indeed, to support your actual research. You will still have contact during your study with the eminent personage but you are less likely to need to wait for long periods for feedback on your work while they attend to other pressing duties across the university or even abroad. It is more important to make contact with, and be supervised by, someone with both expertise and an interest in helping you to develop your research than someone who is especially famous in the area. Though occasionally these qualities of fame, interest and expertise can be found in one person, a team is the more likely way of achieving the complete combination of attributes. In addition, it is becoming increasingly common in the UK that the quality assurance mechanisms of HEIs require each research student to be supported by a team of supervisors to ensure continuity of support for students. Each institution uses and/or defines teams in various ways – indeed there may be differences between departments within an institution – but the objective is always to provide intellectual and pastoral support consistently, whatever the other duties and demands on the academics involved.

ACTIVITY 5 IDENTIFYING POTENTIAL RESEARCH CONTACTS

Consider the names and affiliations of the authors who seem to be currently working in your field, selecting out those who work in institutions that might be accessible to you and with whom it might be useful to make initial contact to register your research interest. Construct a list of Potential Research Contacts.

Next, investigate the institutions in which they work (or worked at the time of publishing the book or article you read) and check whether there are other members of staff who might also be added to your list.

Update your list as you read and attend research conferences, not neglecting those people who live abroad in case they might be useful contacts at a later stage.

Prospective students of EU origin may have to fulfil three-year residency requirements for some funding awards while those who do not meet this requirement may qualify for 'fees only' awards, so they will have to find other resources for living costs and for other research costs such as travel and equipment. Some students seek loans, draw on family resources or their own savings, or seek employment to supplement their income but be careful to check on any restrictions imposed by those paying the fees on the number of hours of paid work allowed alongside research obligations. Obviously they will expect you to complete your study within a specified time so they do not countenance untoward distractions from research. Another possibility for EU and also some overseas prospective students to consider is enrolment in a local university with a view to seeking support for an exchange fellowship in another country of their choice. This is particularly useful when conducting research with an international dimension.

While some UK institutions offer scholarships to international students, in general or from specific countries, if you are in this category but also seeking other sources of support, do take into account that the fees for overseas students are full-cost fees to cover things like infrastructure costs that are to some extent subsidised for home students (at the time of writing) by the UK government. Also, you must take account of the high cost of living in the UK for which stipends may be barely adequate, especially if you choose an institution in a high rent or very cold area (most good institutions in the UK will be in either one or both of these situations). If you are seeking funding for research based in a Higher Education institution in your own country outside the UK, then what has been said to this point about assiduous preliminary research about the host institution and their provision and about the needs and requirements of funding providers will apply to you equally because funding is scarce and competition high in all countries for such places. In Appendix 1 some references are provided to set you on the track of Private and Public Foundations in other countries, particularly North America.

SECURING A PLACE ON A HIGHER DEGREE BY RESEARCH PROGRAMME

As we said in the preface, one of the inspirations for writing this book came from the responses we had from colleagues when we asked them about what the important functions were of research proposals and what they expected them to contain. Although there was some variation in responses in relation to length, sections and detail of content, all of them included and described two overarching aims of a proposal for admission to a *research degree* in their discipline, which generally had equal importance.

The first relates to what purpose writing a proposal serves for the prospective student while the second refers to what purpose the proposal serves for the institution (or rather the academics reviewing it).

From the perspectives of experienced academics, the very process of writing, whether it be a proposal or an essay or any other similar task, is the first and essential step not simply to putting thoughts in order but also in recognising what your thoughts are. The practical task of writing (here we mean either handwriting or typing) forces all of us to confront the ephemeral notions that twist and weave within our minds, translate them into words and then into phrases that might convey meaning to other people. We will deal in the next chapter with syntax and grammar and other such devices for helping us to convey meaning more accurately, because here the focus is on accessing for yourself the complexity of what you have in mind. One of us, when completing her own doctoral studies about the value of figurative language in explanation, was fortunate enough to come across a short poem (Read, 1981, in Hofstadter, 1985) that expressed succinctly a notion that she had had while writing up, and that poem has become increasingly relevant the more she has learnt, researched and been engaged in teaching and supervising others. Its special message, contained in a metaphor about the full, living beauty of fluttering butterflies being lost when they are captured, killed and pinned down on boards by collectors, resonates with what our colleagues tried to convey in different ways about the writing process.

So writing the proposal will help you to pin down more precisely what you want to do and why, to identify your interests and what you already know. In addition, it also reveals what more you need to know and stimulates further thought about how you might find that out. Furthermore, this should contribute to raising your confidence that the task ahead, while difficult, is feasible with a fair wind and appropriate support. Once those ideas have been crystallised into words, it enables the person who receives your proposal, usually a senior academic within a school or department in charge of postgraduate research studies, to identify whether or not there are one or more members of academic staff who share your interests and have expertise in both the topic and research support who might be interested in becoming your supervisor/advisor and have the time to do so.

This is an important part of the preliminary steps on the way to being accepted as a research student. There must be someone, and nowadays more usually a team, who can guide and support your work within the institution. As we indicated earlier, you should do your homework in advance of finally submitting your application, to check on the existence of such people by looking at staff research profiles on web pages and/or in prospectuses. At the same time you should also recognise that someone you suspect of having the relevant qualifications may already have other work commitments which mean that they cannot immediately take on another research student. Most good research institutions have work-load models to ensure that staff have time for research and so that their research students can expect not to be neglected. It is to your advantage that this is the case but it can be disappointing not to gain a place on your chosen academic's research team. That is why it is sensible that you remain flexible, open to suggestions, and also to have several options in mind yourself.

Taking on a research student, and a candidate for doctoral study in particular, is a large and serious undertaking for supervisors and for departments/schools and institutions. They will be investing not only a lot of resources, especially time, in this enterprise but also their reputation because, while a successful outcome brings kudos, added networks and so on, having a research student who does not succeed reflects on their own research and supervision skills and hence standing in the academic community. They are also aware of how much the potential student will be investing: personal **credibility**, sense of worth, status in their family and perhaps at work and in their social community, as well as time and money (actual and opportunity costs). Taking on a new research student is therefore an absolutely critical decision. While there are many unknowns, as any prediction about the future includes, they thus seek good evidence that presages a satisfactory outcome before committing to the undertaking. They seek the first layer of that evidence in your initial proposal. If this captures their attention then an **interview** may follow and thereafter help with developing the proposal to attract funding, if that is feasible.

SECTIONS WITHIN A PROPOSAL – WHAT FUNDERS OR RESEARCH DEGREE REVIEWERS ARE LOOKING FOR

We will provide here a brief overview of the proposal in terms of what university selectors are looking for in a potentially suitable candidate and what funders are seeking in a person and piece of research they could invest in. (More detail about the review process is included in Chapter 9.) Thus, you can begin to get a feel for the whole enterprise of proposal writing before proceeding to examine the particular sections of a proposal, which are dealt with more fully in subsequent chapters. Earlier we emphasised the need to check, in this competitive environment, the specific requirements of your target audience and we are repeating it again because each Higher Education Institution and each funding body has developed, over the period of their existence, idiosyncratic requirements in relation to what and how much they want to know at this stage, the order in which they would like it presented and the form in which they prefer it to be. In responding exactly to these requirements you are taking the first steps in demonstrating the research skills of:

- seeking appropriate information;
- attending to detail;
- considering your audience in your presentation.

You are also demonstrating respect for and interest in the person/institution/organisation you are applying to – put yourself in the shoes of someone who receives a great many applications and who comes across one that is clearly a copy of a proposal sent out to several others, using a scatter-gun technique. Would you bother inspecting and analysing it to find the information you need, possibly embedded in more that you do not? Further, imagine how annoyed and thus unsympathetic that person might be if some particular piece of information they require is not readily apparent or is not presented in the way they request in their literature.

The diversity exhibited between HEIs is also mirrored within them, so, although there is likely to be an institutional form to complete with information about yourself and your proposed research (in hardcopy, typed or handwritten, or in electronic format), there will be specific requirements of your proposal that differ between disciplines. This is matched in the funding arena with some requiring, for instance, *preliminary expressions of interest* while others expect a full proposal with specified sections, each with a fixed word allowance. Yet others require varying degrees of structure and formality in between those extremes.

In many science, technology and engineering disciplines, for instance, whether you are responding to a call for proposals or submitting a speculative one, the topic of your work will need to fit into a specific area of the field that is currently a priority for the funder or, in an HEI, is currently being explored by staff and their team of research students. In a specific institution, while there should be room for further 'moulding to fit' of your personal contribution to the general research project of the team, it is unlikely that equipment and materials will be available for a very different topic even if the expertise required is. However, in disciplines that are less dependent on expensive hardware or consumables such as most mathematical or arts, humanities or social science disciplines, academics in these fields are much more open to, and often relish, a proposal to explore something unique and different, albeit still within their range of expertise. Similarly, funders of research in these fields are likely to consider a greater range of topics within a more broadly defined priority area. Importantly, all recipients of your proposal will be looking for that special quality of distinctiveness, that special something that makes your bid stand out for consideration above the many others they receive.

Differences in how much they want to know is not so readily categorised by discipline. Some will specify a succinct summary with a single paragraph accorded to each section (see below), while others will expect a more detailed accounting of each area. Some will provide headings while others will expect you to demonstrate that you know what features are required within a research proposal – see Box 1.

MAIN FEATURES OF PROPOSALS

BOX 1 MAIN FEATURES OF A PROPOSAL

All reviewers will expect you, amongst other things, to demonstrate:

- a knowledge of the field;
- awareness of what might be an original focus within it;
- intellectual rigour;
- an understanding of the need to communicate clearly and an ability to articulate ideas;
- an ability to organise ideas and plan work;
- an appreciation of the potential value of the outcomes;
- attention to the feasibility;
- attention to sustainability;
- and the cost effectiveness of the project.

Evidence for these skills and attributes can be woven into headings of your choice or included under any provided section labels. Please be especially alert, though, that when a word length is specified, it is usually strongly adhered to, anything beyond it being ignored or even elided from the form if it is electronically submitted. This means that you have to craft your sections carefully to ensure that all these points are included appropriately somewhere, within the boundaries given. The aspects that should be covered in one form or another, under one heading or another, are included in Box 2. The refinements in brackets refer to the situation in which you are speculatively seeking a research degree place while the main statements refer to both degree place and funding proposals.

BOX 2 IMPORTANT ASPECTS OF A PROPOSAL

- A title that encapsulates the key aspects of the proposal in a few key words.
- A statement of the aims/purpose of the research with objectives identified (at least in a preliminary way).
- The research questions or hypotheses (at least in speculative form, to be refined as the research progresses).
- A (preliminary) review of the relevant literature that indicates that you are familiar with the field and have identified some gap/s that your proposed research will address. This

(Continued)

(Continued)

should also identify the (general) theoretical framework which will be applied to your research and indicate your ability to evaluate the work of others.

- A section that describes (in outline) the methodology proposed, that is, a rationale for the approach, design and methods, and a plan, with timings, for how they will be implemented. This should encompass any model you intend to test and what kind of **data** you plan to collect and why, as well as how you will analyse it.
- It is usual too to include a budget (or a list of essential resources and where/how they might be accessed). Some funders require (and potential supervisors will appreciate) a consideration of any barriers to completion that might occur and how these could be overcome. (This is a lot of important information and so might well be covered by several sections rather than just one.)
- A section that speculates about potential outcomes and their value/potential impact.
- A list of references with full bibliographic detail.

In a proposal for a *research degree* some institutions or departments prefer the proposal to be set out like chapters in an eventual thesis (perhaps: Introduction, Literature Review, Methodology, Research Design and Methods, Discussion of Results, Potential Conclusions, References), with a brief summary in each of the proposed final content.

Some funders and most applications for a research degree will expect a covering letter to accompany the formal research proposal and the nature of this will be an important topic, along with ideas for refining the title of your proposal, in the next chapter where we will focus on the tone, tenor and style of writing that are required of research proposals, or at least that will help it gain positive attention. The chapters that come after will explore the sections of the proposal in some detail but for now we have included in Box 3 a summary of evidence required when applying for a research degree place and in Box 4 a review of the different mechanisms that are used to gain financial support for such studies.

BOX 3 EVIDENCE TO BE INCLUDED IN RESEARCH DEGREE PROPOSALS

- Each HEI has its own 'application for postgraduate research study' procedures but most require, in addition to or included in the application form, a research project outline, and evidence of readiness for undertaking independent research, including degree transcripts and references from academic and perhaps professional sources.

- Some disciplines require evidence of writing or creative ability in the form of essays or a portfolio of work.
- International students will always be required to provide evidence of a good standard of English language though actual qualification levels differ between disciplines and institutions. Such students will also be required to meet conditions for a student visa (note: these conditions are currently being revised and potential applicants should check the UK Border Agency website).
- Prospective students will also need to furnish evidence of adequate funding for fees and maintenance.

BOX 4 MECHANISMS FOR FINANCING A RESEARCH DEGREE

- Self-funding: Study and personal maintenance costs funded through savings, family contributions, private loans and/or paid employment. Note that institutions may have formal or informal restrictions on the number of hours of employment allowed for students registered as full time. There is very limited access to paid employment within institutions and this varies by discipline as well as by institution.
- Employer supported: Unless the research project has been specifically commissioned by the employer, full support from employers is unusual though some may pay fees as part of staff development policy or may provide support in kind, such as regular paid study leave.
- Collaborative studentships: Occasionally universities or research institutes co-fund doctoral study with another organisation, such as a hospital or pharma company. The particular arrangements will be detailed in advertised studentships.
- Institutional funding: A range of funding opportunities exist at either institution or school/department level ranging from full support of fees and stipend through a scholarship or bursary to a simple fee waiver scheme. These will be advertised in prospectuses and websites.
- Charitable trusts: Again support from these sources varies from small-scale financial support for conference attendance to full fee and stipend, though the latter is rare, and there are likely to be very specific criteria to be met, such as residency or professional experience requirements. Information on these sources can be found in Appendix 1.
- Research council funding (UK): The vast majority of this funding is allocated through particular institutions through specific studentships. In the past there have also been a few studentships available through open competition although still requiring preliminary institutional acceptance. This situation is currently changing so details should be checked on relevant websites (see Appendix 1).
- Overseas funding sources – check with the International Offices in institutions and see Appendix 1.

REFLECTION POINT: EXPLORING POTENTIAL AUDIENCES AND THEIR REQUIREMENTS

Consider what you know about the specific audiences for your proposal, what more you need to know and how that information will influence what you include in your proposal, what you exclude and how you approach developing it.

3

WHAT ARE THE KEY ASPECTS OF PROPOSAL PREPARATION?

CHAPTER OVERVIEW

This chapter discusses:

- the key orientating concepts of proposals;
- the content and form of the title, abstract, covering letter (if required) and supporting documents;
- choosing a style of writing appropriate for the readership;
- developing drafts in the appropriate register, voice and verb tense;
- describing the **conceptual framework** and producing a sound argument;
- advance planning of proposal production.

PRE-PREPARATION

It must be clear by now that the process of preparing a proposal is not simply sitting down and writing about what you want to do and why. It does include that, but only as a small proportion of what needs to be done, while the actual final draft writing will come last after many other activities. This can be a frustrating experience especially if this is your first venture into proposal development; understandably you will want to be seeing some progress. It might help if you view this proposal as a mini-research project in itself, requiring all the elements of drafting aims, reviewing relevant documents, re-drafting aims, formalising research questions/hypotheses, designing method and including a time plan of activities, before the actual research (or in this simile, proposal writing) can take place. By this point you will have recognised that, if you are not to waste your time and that of others, dedicating time and effort to the preparation stage is essential. If a submission deadline is approaching rapidly, then you have two options, of which putting in a 'quick and dirty' bid should not be one. (This would be unlikely to enhance your reputation with the reviewers, and the disappointment of a rejection will not help your confidence.) The two options are that, if possible, you set other tasks and chores aside so that you can devote concentrated attention to doing a really good job with the proposal, or that you defer submission until the next round, even if it is a year away, so that you can organise well by starting on the preparations in a timely manner. Your circumstances and stamina will be the determinants of which of these you choose.

For now, let us begin to help you see ways in which you can make tangible progress by reviewing some of the key points from the previous chapter, each of which requires some productive activity from you.

ACTIVITY 6 CRITICAL QUESTIONS AND ANSWERS FOR PROPOSAL DEVELOPMENT

Some important messages that require responses from the previous chapter include:

Research topic – this may be completely your own idea or you may be putting your own personal perspective onto a topic area selected by others. Check which of these applies to your current proposal and how that might influence your next steps. In particular, identify the general topics that are currently in vogue and attracting attention and seek out other trustworthy peers who are interested and have expertise in the area to discuss your ideas.

Types of research – this depends on what you are trying to achieve with the research and will affect how it is viewed by those individuals within organisations whose support you need to finance it or provide facilities and intellectual support for it. Consider if a particular purpose underpins your desire to engage in a particular research type and how that meshes with your abilities and opportunities.

Sources of funding – no research project is totally cost free. There will certainly be opportunity costs in relation to your time, and even the least technical research is likely to involve, as a minimum, IT facilities, possible travel to libraries and some book and stationery purchases. At the other end of the spectrum, you may need to negotiate and fund access to extremely expensive equipment and consumables as well as secure financial support for living, fees and other research expenses. Explore all the possible sources of funding that may be available, perhaps building a portfolio of those that apply particularly to your area so that you will have a resource for now and the future. In the interest of your current project, start to build a strategy to acquire enough resources, from one or more sources, bearing in mind that that a practicable and cost-effective proposal is most likely to appeal to funders.

Expert support – whether you are a prospective student or a member of staff seeking research funding, wise counselling and practical support from another research colleague will be invaluable in preparing a successful proposal. Begin to identify these potential helpers/mentors, considering how and when it would be best to make contact.

The value of writing while preparing – it is never too soon to start drafting ideas, turning fleeting **constructs** into more permanent forms so that you can look at them more carefully. The need for great care becomes obvious when considering what the reader is seeking from the document – firm evidence that further engagement with you will be worthwhile. Consider ways in which you might engage your audience then see if we can add to your own ideas in this and the following chapters.

The structure of the proposal – different stakeholders in research, particularly funders and academic reviewers, are all looking both for distinctiveness in a proposal, what makes it shine out from amongst other applications, and conformity to rigorous criteria in research practice. In other words, they are seeking the contrasting attributes of uniqueness of topic and potential originality of results alongside adherence to traditional values and recognisable pathways. There are similarities and differences between potential audiences in their requirements. Some will provide stringent guidelines for the structuring of your proposal while others will check to see if you can encompass what is required in an accessible form of your own devising. Check the published requirements of your audience/s so that you can then evaluate which of the ideas presented in later chapters will best suit your purpose and their need.

Additional things to check carefully in the information given out by funders or research degree providers are any *eligibility criteria* and what guidance they give about requirements for *referees*. It would be a pity to waste effort on devising a proposal for a situation in which you do not meet the eligibility criteria, which may be residence requirements or the possession of a particular degree, for instance. If you think you might have a good case for a slight variation in the requirements, then do contact the organisation to discuss this possibility before expending too much effort only to be disappointed. We will follow up about referees in more detail in Chapter 9 when we explore the selection of potential referees for formal review of the final product and the value of critical friends for informal review and feedback in the preparation process.

Having begun to gather together all of this 'intelligence' from outside sources, you should now be eager to begin the writing task proper, as opposed to making notes, and, if you are new to research, then you may be exercised by trying to start off by writing the *title*. Although this looks like a natural beginning and is the first thing the recipient will read of your formal proposal, it is wise to resist spending more than a few minutes on this early in your writing; instead devise a working title that will keep you focussed on what you intend to do. This may change as you prepare your full proposal and you will find it easier to review and hone your working title than one to which you have committed prematurely. The same applies to any *abstract* that may be required and indeed any *covering letter*. All of these are best written when you have completed and polished the main proposal, because its content will inform these other three parts, providing key words and critical aspects of the proposed research. However, we will provide here some guidance on these three elements, referring back to them in the final chapter, so that you can be contemplating them at the back of your mind for future refinement when the time is ripe.

THE TITLE, ABSTRACT AND COVERING LETTER

First, please note that both the title and abstract may be restricted in size, with some funders specifying even the number of letters and spaces in the title and a maximum number of words in the abstract. Again this calls for a careful review of the organisation's regulations. Even when no guidance is given, both the title and abstract do need to combine the virtues of succinctness, accuracy and attractiveness. In fact, all writing in research should aim to be concise, precise and elegant, although these are not easily achieved independently so are even more difficult in combination. This takes much practice but we will provide some further guidelines later to help you. While working on other aspects of your proposal keep a note of key words, phrases and concepts that best express what you are doing, why and how, and with which expected result. These are the components that must be expressed in your title in a form that compels the reader to keep on reading. You may find that keeping a small notepad in your pocket or bag is useful for recording that bright idea that pops into your head at unexpected moments, in a queue, on a train or while peeling potatoes!

The abstract should follow up the title by providing even more clues to the reader that the rest of the document contains information that will be interesting and useful to her/him. It should summarise in a few sentences the aim of the research, the approach and methods and expected outcomes. It should indicate what needs will be met by the research through the application of appropriate investigation. Some funding agencies require a 'lay' abstract as well as, or instead of, a professional one. Such an abstract is intended to summarise the research for someone whose background is not in that specific area, so this adds an extra requirement on your writing skills to banish any disciplinary or research-oriented idiom in the interest of knowledge transfer. Often the word limit for abstracts is between 250 and 350 words. (This whole paragraph is about 300 words long.) Writing within these confines is not easy and all of us, no matter how experienced, take several drafts to get a particular abstract and title just right. One first tip is to avoid superfluous words in the title such as 'An Investigation of …'. or 'A Project to'; instead go straight to 'The effect on X of Y, using Z' or 'A comparison of X and Y in Z conditions', for example. You may find it helpful to review some titles and abstracts in your own discipline by consulting scholarly journals and by accessing recently completed projects within the websites of your funding body/ies. This will be the best indicator of what style and content is currently successful and will also provide examples from your field of ways of expressing complex ideas. Remember that, although you want to grab your reader's attention, this is a sophisticated audience so avoid the temptation to use overly emotive words and exclamation marks.

You can ensure that your passion for research shines through in other ways such as producing well-evidenced research problems addressed by careful **research designs**, sensitive to context, facilities, budgets and any participants, or **subjects**, involved.

Being sensitive to your audience is also critical if your proposal requires a covering letter. This requirement is becoming less common when responding to calls for proposals because electronic formats for submission are becoming increasingly popular with funding agencies. However, they can be very helpful if corresponding with agencies to whom you may be making a speculative bid or with university departments in which you want to study. A covering letter provides an opportunity for you to make personal contact (even if a relatively formal style is required), to introduce yourself and the suitability of your skills and commitment, demonstrate your interest in the recipient, exemplify your writing skills and engage their attention. Your proposal will get no further if this letter creates a bad impression so it is worthwhile spending some time on it to strike the right note. Layout is important: it should be tidy, clean, with clear type and legible font, and use professional conventions. These include addressing the letter to a specific named person wherever possible, and getting their personal title correct (check the website and/or ring up the secretary to check – use only the specific job title in extremis). It should conclude with 'Yours sincerely,' with your name typed below your signature.

The body of the letter should first state who you are and your purpose in sending the letter – referring to any enclosures (your proposal, CV and so forth). It is also a good idea to put 'ENCLOSURE/S' (as appropriate) at the bottom of the page so that they do not get omitted if the letter is forwarded to another department. While being brief and to the point, flag up what you want to draw the organisation's attention to, for instance, the particular suitability of your background for the project. It can be beneficial too if you can demonstrate at the same time that you have made an effort to explore the organisation's mission and objectives. Thus you can, without simply bragging, explain that you have a skill or approach or personal attribute that fits in with their culture and goals. For example:

> The skills of questionnaire design I developed in my Masters' research project, and the complimentary feedback I received from the examiners, fit well with the types of project you outline in your prospectus/call for bids.

Or:

> It is clear from your documentation that xxxxx is required of researchers in this field. My CV demonstrates that this is an attribute that I have cultivated fruitfully over the last few years.

Take care not to claim anything that is not backed up by your CV and/or proposal. Further, all of these documents should be consistent in style and presentation to demonstrate your organisational abilities and your respect for the importance and formality of the occasion. Because you may be sending your proposal to several recipients, do not forget to adapt it to what you have learned about the culture, requirements and style of each one and then ensure that your letter and abstract also fit well with the idiosyncrasies of each. For instance, you can include a paragraph that is tailored to each recipient along the lines of:

> 'I note with interest your emphasis on . . .' or 'Projects that you have funded recently are related to this proposal in that . . .'

Check whether they need such documents as an up-to-date CV, original degree certificates, transcripts of your degree and the formal results of any English Language test, if applicable. All of these except for the CV are more likely to be required at a later stage in the process than the first submission of your proposal but ensuring they are ready to hand is part of your preparation. Finally, if you are unused to writing formal letters then you might find it helpful to visit the careers office in your current organisation for advice, or you could find some further guidelines and examples on the website for the Graduate Recruitment Bureau (www.grb.uk.com).

THE BODY OF THE PROPOSAL – AUDIENCE AND STYLE

Once again, knowing your audience is critical for setting the correct tone, using the most appropriate language and marketing your ideas effectively. In general, you should have an image of your reader as being an educated generalist, not an expert in your particular niche of your academic field. Often proposals go through a sifting procedure with the first level being someone who decides not just which expert should see it next but also whether it should go forward at all. Therefore it is important to avoid all of the pitfalls noted in Box 5.

BOX 5 WHAT TO AVOID IN FORMAL WRITING

- Jargon – this is irritating and unnecessary.
- Waffle – the reviewer will stop reading and move on to another proposal.
- Elaborate sentence construction – clarity should be your aim.
- Acronyms or initials without a full-text version first that has acronym or initials in brackets.
- Abbreviations commonly used in informal writing such as 'sha'n't' or 'we'll'.
- Overly sophisticated or obscure words – the reader will not be impressed if they cannot understand you or think you are trying to be smart.
- Informalities and over-personalisation such as 'I am not convinced', 'from my perspective' – this is a formal document that requires an argument constructed with evidence rather than simply opinion.

Engaging in research is a professional commitment and there is a whole section of the Researcher Development Framework (see Chapter 1) that emphasises skill in communication. You therefore need to demonstrate to your well-educated reader that you can write in a form that describes your proposal in clear terms, using words that paint a picture and give insight into your thinking. You need to structure the story in a logical way that leads the reader through the process, providing signposts and using any headings that are demanded or recommended in the organisation's guidance notes. You need to be persuasive that the problem your research will address exists, or that a need has arisen for the focus of your research and that your approach is both viable and sensible. If you are seeking funding then you need to convince the reader that you are a worthy recipient while if you are seeking a degree place you need to satisfy the authorities that you have the right credentials and potential.

DEVELOPING YOUR PROPOSAL DRAFT

You would be a very unusual person, a paragon of research, if you were able to achieve all of those things in the first draft and, in the interest of brevity, include not one superfluous word. Therefore be prepared for an iterative or recursive process in which you draft, review, re-draft, have it proof-read by another, re-draft and edit, have it checked by colleague or expert in the field, then attend to required amendments. It is easy to fall into the various traps of being shy to show your first attempts, to be precious about your whole idea or particular expressions of it, or to worry about bothering others, but, as we will advise in a later chapter, soliciting others' views on your drafts is the essence of collegiate research and actually standard practice in academia. It is recognised that it is relatively easier to spot grammatical or typographical errors in the work of others than to notice such things in your own, while better ways to express things can emerge once the crux of the idea is presented. Equally, no one expects you to be an absolute expert on every aspect of your topic so sharing your writing with others will result in their giving you new ideas or leads, or suggesting alternative ways of looking at things – just as your writing will have added to their portfolio of understanding.

There are, though, some practical ways in which you can help yourself to get a good draft together before sharing it with others. These should ensure that what you say:

- avoids misinterpretation of the meaning;
- has the right word used at the right time without being too repetitive;
- is expressed in an accessible and digestible form;
- contains ideas that are expressed coherently and imaginatively;
- attracts the eye;
- makes sense as a whole (see Box 6).

BOX 6 PRACTICAL POINTS FOR WRITING

- Keep beside you a dictionary to check on meanings of words.
- Have to hand a thesaurus to find alternative, perhaps more accurate, words.
- Use bullet points for lists to make them stand out.
- Keep your paragraphs short and focussed.
- Insert headings and sub-headings to guide the reader.
- Use diagrams, tables, graphs and illustrations that summarise points or convey how they are linked.
- Employ italics and bold sparingly and with purpose but avoid underlining.
- Make it visually pleasing by ensuring the type face and font are easy to read and consistent.
- Do not trust electronic spell checkers – they only spot non-words not wrong words.
- Polish, hone and craft your sentences.
- Read your work out loud – it might be a bit embarrassing to be caught doing so but it will help you spot mistakes, non sequiturs and sentences that are too convoluted.

LANGUAGE REGISTER, VOICE AND VERB TENSE

Another issue that causes some debate is the language register you should use, more particularly whether a proposal should be in the first or third person ('I/we' or 'the investigator/researcher/student') and whether verbs should be in active or passive mode (e.g. 'we will interview/conduct an **experiment**', 'we have shown' as opposed to 'an interview/experiment will be conducted', 'it was shown'). In the past the traditions of the humanities, the social sciences and the sciences differed, passive voice being preferred in the sciences (for example, rather than write, 'I conducted an experiment', the format would be, 'An experiment was conducted'). A colleague in the School of Modern Languages tells us that there is a cliché in French academia that 'one should not use "I" until one has grey hair'. In contrast, in most of the social sciences it is considered either quite clumsy or unnecessarily pedantic when writing about what you did to use the form: 'The investigator will conduct an interview . . .'. Remember that now the general preference is for accessible, simple and effective writing so avoid cumbersome phrases when a simple statement can be used such as 'I will conduct an interview'.

On the other hand, try to counter any charge of egomania by using the passive voice when it fits well in the flow of the text, such as 'In this case an interview will be used to . . .'. Sometimes it helps (or it may be common in the field – check any accessible, recent, successful proposals in your area) to use the plural version, especially in the sciences when a laboratory team is to be involved in the project, such as 'we have previously explored'. Whichever version you chose, be consistent across similar occasions, so that if you refer to work you did in the past (usually with someone's help), use 'we', while if you are referring to an activity you will undertake entirely alone in the future use 'I' or the passive voice, if that fits the context.

In many discipline areas it is now standard procedure to use the past tense for findings in the literature, no matter how recently published, such as, 'these researchers suggested . . .'; the present tense for the rationale, 'There is little evidence that . . .'; the predictive tense for anticipated methods, 'an experimental approach will . . .'; and the conditional 'may' to refer to possible outcomes. Although you cannot promise specific outcomes, because you would not be proposing to do research if the outcomes were obvious, you should not be too diffident about the results. Instead suggest that, whatever the specific results, the outcome will be a useful contribution to illuminating the research problem.

If you missed out on grammar lessons, particularly punctuation and syntax, in your early schooling, or if English is not your first language, then it is more important than ever to get support from a proof-reader who is very good at English. This need not be the same person who reviews your drafts for technical points but rather one who will advise you on expressing yourself well. We will suggest at the end of the book, in Appendix 2, some self-help texts so that you can improve your own performance, but we recognise that this is a gradual process in which you will improve with practice and feedback. One very good but simple habit to get into is to write while the muse is with you, then put it away for a few days and review it. You are then more likely to see what is really written there rather than what you thought you had conveyed. Professional writers like us always do that – and often cannot believe what we have written – and then we ask each other to proof-read it again. It is always a relief when a 'trusted other' spots something that evaded our own eagle eyes.

Before we leave the topic of which words to use, it is important to provide a link through the words you use to the mission statements, research priorities and strategic aims of the organisation you are approaching. In the literature of psychology this is known as a form of 'echoing' that helps to build rapport by demonstrating familiarity with your prospective partner, which is useful in itself. In addition, using this technique will indicate to you whether you are indeed on the right track. If you find it difficult to use some of the key words and phrases from the organisation's documents in your proposal, or if you cannot work out what they mean, then it is unlikely that your argument will sound convincing to your readers.

THE CONCEPTUAL FRAMEWORK

A convincing argument is just what you need in the main body of your proposal. It will be persuasive if you attend to the points made in Box 7.

BOX 7 HOW TO PRODUCE AN INFLUENTIAL ARGUMENT – THE CONCEPTUAL FRAMEWORK

You should:

- identify the problem;
- provide evidence for the need for the research;
- state its aims and objectives clearly and precisely;
- clarify the research hypotheses or questions that emerge from the aims and objectives;
- describe your intentions;
- justify, with evidence of appropriateness, the methods you will use to satisfy the aims;
- propose a realistic budget;
- design an **evaluation** of the process;
- discuss the value of the projected outcome and outputs.

In the USA, the first few steps constitute what is termed a 'needs statement'. In all contexts, this is the part of the proposal that sets the scene for the rest of the research and which much be substantiated by using well-referenced sources, quoting authorities on the topic and, if appropriate, statistics that demonstrate the parameters of the problem. As you will have guessed by now, it is wise to check on the referencing convention favoured by your audience but, by and large, unless one is specified in the guidance material, any standard referencing system will be acceptable if it is used consistently. Again you are demonstrating to the reviewer that you have the skills required of a researcher.

You will also need to justify, again referring to authoritative texts, your planned procedure for investigating the topic and for evaluating your process. You should be able to find opportunities in these sections in which to introduce a flow chart or diagram which can condense many words into a clear illustration of process. More detail about what to include in these sections and on devising and presenting the budget will be provided in the chapters that follow.

Finally, remember that this is a competitive process so ensure, even after you have observed all the requirements and revised your writing over and over again, that your proposal conveys the commitment you intend to bring to the research. Do not polish out the sense of excitement that you should be bringing to this activity. This is what will sustain you and the research project through the inevitable difficulties that arise, and reviewers will need some reassurance that such a spark exists. The 'inevitable difficulties' may not always be apparent in the 'authoritative texts' in your literature review, which we turn to in the next chapter, but are a normal part of any research project.

ACTIVITY 7 LEARNING FROM EXAMPLES OF PREVIOUS SUCCESSFUL PROPOSALS

Before you get to that chapter, add to your list of 'things to do soon' an exploration of previously successful proposals, reflecting particularly on the writing style and format. The best of these resources in terms of currency and topicality will be those most recently submitted and funded in your department or school (for those already established in one) or supported by your favoured funding body. Check, therefore, your local resource base or library and relevant websites (Appendix 1).

In Appendix 2, we have provided an annotated bibliography of books that provide help with English, guidance on referencing and examples of a range of proposals,

(Continued)

(Continued)

though these will only be indicators of style approved at a time before publication of the work.

If you have access to a university library then seek out your discipline librarian for advice on where to access examples of past proposals or final reports.

Check the websites, in Appendix 1, of the funding agencies supporting your discipline for titles and abstracts of current projects and reports from previous ones.

REFLECTION POINT: WORDS TO STRUCTURE YOUR ARGUMENT

Your proposal is in essence an argument that should be authoritative but not arrogant. Consider the following sample list of verbs and how they could be used to construct your argument.

Document; demonstrate; establish; explore; identify; determine; develop; propose; posit; define; report; assess; critique; integrate; compare; contrast; review; discover; disclose; evidence; evaluate; suggest; appraise; contribute; conjecture.

You can add to this list as you read through examples of proposals in your field so that you have to hand an aide-mémoire of relevant and appropriate words.

STAGES IN THE PRODUCTION OF THE PROPOSAL – ADVANCE PLANNING

From the outline presented in the Prologue, and the fact that a whole book has been devoted to the multiple aspects of a proposal, you will not have failed to realise that another of the attributes you will need for a future in research, whether you are starting out on a *research degree* or looking for *funding for research,* is good organisational ability. You can demonstrate this attribute by planning the development, execution and completion of the research proposal (the research in theory) and then doing the same for the actual project (the research in practice). We will explore project planning in detail in Chapter 8 but here we will introduce the tasks you need to complete and then consider how long they might take and their order of execution to produce a proposal that stands a good chance of success.

The first thing to do is make a list of everything you need to do from:

> registering onto paper either the impulse/compulsion to do some research or the actual germ of an idea for a research topic,

to:

> submitting your proposal in hard copy or by an electronic submission process, whichever is required by the organisation involved.

We cannot be prescriptive about what might be on this list as it will depend on a multiplicity of things, such as where you are on the dimensions in Box 8, which contains possible starting points.

BOX 8 HOW TO PLOT YOUR STARTING POINT

It may be that:

- you are hoping to register for a degree or to gain financial support to undertake research;
- you are familiar with only a few or a potentially large number of research support organisations/institutions;
- you have little or no experience of research or a more substantial amount;
- you intend working on a topic about which your knowledge of relevant literature is extensive or limited;
- your network of academic guides, mentors and helpful colleagues is well established or is yet only wished for;
- the topic itself fits within a well-researched field or is distinctly novel and under-researched;
- you are conversant with a wide range of research approaches and techniques or need to explore these further;
- the topic generates questions or hypotheses that fit comfortably within your experience of research or demand new perspectives;

and so on.

Where you sit on each of these dimensions will guide you about what more you need to do in relation to them for the particular proposal you envisage. In addition, the aspects of a proposal listed in Box 2, the important tasks you considered in Activity 6 and the conceptual framework that you found in Box 7, alongside the chapter headings and sub-headings in this book will contribute many of the items in your personal list of things that you need to do.

ACTIVITY 8 ADVANCE PLANNING ACTIVITY

Start to draft your personal list of the activities you will need to undertake in order to produce a strong proposal. You might like to brainstorm all the possibilities that come to mind right away, then check through the sources mentioned above to add any you missed, or instead go methodically through those sources noting all the aspects and tasks and then review the list for repetitions.

Next, consider the order in which you need to undertake the necessary activities. Some will be natural precursors to others; others must take place later in the process. One simple way to sort these is to write the activities on separate Post-it notes then shuffle them round until you get the best order. As you begin to put them in sequence you are likely to discover that some will overlap with others or, indeed, should take place simultaneously. There are some activities that spread across a period of time during which several others take place, one such being the literature review, which needs to be kept up to date once the main sources have been identified. You could present this as a hierarchical chart which begins at the top of the page and works its way down. Alternatively, you might prefer a flow chart with the activities contained in a series of boxes with arrows showing how one activity leads into one or more others, flowing from left to right across the page. In Chapter 8 we will introduce another way of presenting organisational details; by then it will be in the form of a chart of your research-project activities. But we are not quite there yet.

THE CONSTRAINTS OF TIME

The next challenge relates not to what you need do but how long each element might take and what the total time span is, or could be, for producing a good proposal. There are two ways that you can approach this timing issue: either you can determine a fixed amount of time during which you must complete the proposal and then try to fit all the tasks into the space available; or you could judge how long each task or group of tasks might take and then, by adding them together, come up with how much time you will require before submission. In reality, most people find that they are working within one of these general frameworks but having to adjust it to circumstances. So let us assume that you do not have all the time in the world, and that you want to start sometime soon and need to have completed the proposal within a realistic time – perhaps by a closing date for bids or for registration.

This provides the timeline across which you will attempt to fit your flowchart, although do remember our advice at the beginning of the book, that it is better to wait for the next round than waste your time, motivation and self-esteem by putting in an ill-prepared proposal which will inevitably fail and may harm your reputation with the reviewing body. It is also better to realise at this planning stage that you need more time to hone certain skills, make the right contacts and so on than to set your sights on too rapid a completion and be disappointed halfway through that you cannot reach your target date. You may be feeling a little disappointed right now that we are not presenting a quick route to producing a good proposal (we are assuming that you did already know that it would not be an easy route!). But take heart – we will help you to identify and hone the skills that will be needed for the future if you intend to remain a researcher. These skills will improve with practice so that in that future you may indeed be able to produce proposals quite swiftly because you know your own skills, the field of study and the requirements of your main audiences.

At this moment, only you will know where you fit on each of the dimensions we included in Box 8. Therefore we cannot provide you with a pro forma guide to how long each section will take. One thing to make sure of, though, is to allow a good amount of time towards the end of your preparation, and take advice for the submission process from experts in Research Support Offices, especially if electronic submission is required, as is frequently the case nowadays. This is because getting the form exactly right can be tedious and time consuming, even if you have prepared your proposal assiduously in all other respects.

Similarly, we cannot determine the exact order in which you may chose or be able to do such things as make contact with colleagues for various purposes, though we can counsel that you start very early to contact busy people to seek guidance. You will be at the mercy of the availability of people, library books and journals and a myriad of other things which may distract you from your goal. This brings us to noting another of the attributes suggested as essential for the Researcher Development Framework (see Chapter 1) by experts in the field. This attribute was variously labelled determination, stamina, perseverance, persistence, doggedness and so forth by those experts, and we are sure that you are beginning to see now why they said that.

You can help sustain your 'determination . . . and so forth' and save time wasted in confusion by making order out of the complex list of activities that need to be completed to reach your goal. Having a logical flow then enables you to:

- feel secure that important steps have not been missed;
- mark progress as it occurs;
- adapt the order if necessary because new information changes the logic.

ACTIVITY 9 PLOTTING YOUR PROGRESS

Take some time now to draft either a hierarchical list or a flow chart with boxes and arrows to map your progress through the development of a proposal. You could keep this by you as you read and add to it or amend it as you learn more. Indeed, if you are able to engage wholeheartedly with the activities we suggest, then you may find that you have accomplished many of the steps on your chart by the end of the book.

REFLECTION POINT: GIVING LUCK A HAND

It is human when disappointed by our own failure to blame circumstances: we were not given enough time, or luck; we had not realised other alternatives were available; and so on. By now you will realise that we think that you can help luck along and take more control of circumstances, at least where proposal writing is concerned. Keep that in mind as you read further.

4

WHAT SHOULD BE INCLUDED IN THE INTRODUCTION, RATIONALE AND LITERATURE REVIEW?

CHAPTER OVERVIEW

This chapter discusses:

- the reasons for including each of the early sections: introduction, rationale, literature review;
- what each should contain and why;
- details of the requirements of different forms of literature review;
- searching the literature;
- developing your argument.

ORIENTATING THE READER TO YOUR PURPOSE

We are presenting these three topics that feature in proposals – introduction, rationale and literature review – using their most explicitly descriptive titles, because for some purposes and audiences these are potential sections of a document or they may be combined, with any two of them being sub-sections under the heading of the third. Alternatively, they could be presented as 'introduction including a rationale and followed by a literature review' or in some other formulation using such synonyms such as 'background, needs statement and supporting argument'.

Whichever of these is popular in your discipline/culture and for your purpose and audience, the following advice and discussion will be relevant. One of the most important points is that this part of the proposal should be clearly structured to follow a story line that develops an argument supporting your choice of topic and research hypotheses/questions. These latter form the cornerstone of your project and your proposal; indeed, you may be required on funders' forms to declare them before going into further details. Thus they act as a first sift level to reviewers and so should be precise but intriguing. The proposal also needs to demonstrate that they are well-founded and appropriate to context, hence the need for a clear introduction, rationale and sound literature review.

THE INTRODUCTION

It is often helpful to the reader to start the introduction with a clear statement of the overarching purpose of the study and then round off the introduction with its aims and objectives to emphasise the more focussed purpose, again moving from the general to the particular as in the development of the theoretical context, or main review. It is not untoward to include in the introduction to the proposal a short explanation of how your interest in the topic was stimulated, because this also gives you an opportunity to demonstrate how your prior experience and acquired skills make you competent to carry out the research.

If a substantial, rather than preliminary, literature review is required then it is helpful in the introduction to give the reader guidance for the journey, explaining how your argument will develop through the sections and perhaps themes within them.

THE RATIONALE

The development of the conceptual framework for your work demands a transparent rationale. This is where you present your case for the project being a significant enterprise, not simply an interesting question or proposition. Interesting questions abound but the scarcity of funding or of available resources for teaching/research support demands more than the topic being intellectually interesting. There will be an expectation from your reviewers that a worthwhile study will have the potential to contribute to knowledge in a non-trivial way, doing research that has not been done before and producing an outcome which perhaps has significance for policy or practice or both as well as furthering understanding. You have to construct an argument or case that will not disappoint those reviewers so make sure that you not only draw on literature sources that support your choice of purpose and help hone it into specific research questions or hypotheses but also acknowledge and critique those previous writings that contradict your argument or subscribe to an alternative analysis of the situation. This will make your case more convincing and will demonstrate that you are aware of controversies in the field and are not afraid to engage with them.

PREPARING FOR THE LITERATURE REVIEW

Developing this awareness, though, requires a lot of exploration of the literature, frustratingly numerous blind alleys and probably stacks of notes (metaphorical ones on the computer if not in hard copy). So it is wise to begin by adopting a system for storing the reference information in a way that facilitates retrieving aspects of it. In the 'other useful resources' section of Appendix 2 we have noted introductions to the End Note package – this is software for reference management and perhaps one of the most useful electronic methods of storing and retrieving references to date – but if your circumstances demand a low-tech approach then opt for a card-index system that also allows for cross-referencing. (A simple one involves alphabetical author arrangement of index cards in separate boxes for each topic area with perhaps a colour code per topic so that publications dealing with several topics can be readily identified by the multiple colours.) Because any exercise of organising your references marks the beginning of what you hope will be an extensive commitment, it is worthwhile establishing an efficient system early in the process. Any good librarian will be able to advise you on a range of information storage and retrieval devices.

An efficient system for creating a bibliography from which to select your reference lists for different academic purposes includes assiduous attention to detail because you will require page numbers for quotations and full bibliographic detail in references, whichever style you choose or is required by your selected audience. One convention is to provide only the surname/s of the author/s or editor/s with the date of publication in the actual body of the text (e.g. Sparrow, 1999, or Thrush and Swift, 2010, or Pigeon et al., 2009) and a list, entitled 'References', with full reference details in alphabetical order at the end of the proposal. Another convention is to cite the authors or editors with a numerical superscript in the text and a full reference as a correctly numbered footnote on the same page. All referencing conventions will require you to know the authors' (or editors') surnames and initials, the date of publication, the title, the place of publication and the publisher, though the order and style of presentation may vary depending on the system chosen (see Appendix 2 for books on referencing or seek the help of a librarian).

There are conventions to be adhered to also in the way that book chapters, journal articles and internet references are presented. Again, the aid of a librarian with this will be invaluable if an example of the required format is not included with the application details. Attention to detail is a strict requirement, so try not to get irritated when some of your proposal target audiences require full stops after author initials while others do not, because the way you reference your proposal indicates to the reviewers that you will be able and willing to use their preferred convention in your prospective final report.

One particular convention to be alert to is that of seeking out primary sources whenever it is possible. The rationale for this is that you can never be sure that a 'secondary' author has correctly understood and/or accurately quoted the original source; it is all too easy to abstract a sentence or two that seems to support one's argument without paying attention to context and tone. This is a trap that you need to guard against in your own presentation too, because your reviewers may be more familiar with the literature than you are and so spot a misquotation or incorrect attribution.

THE LITERATURE REVIEW ITSELF

For a *research degree proposal*, even one for which you are also seeking funding, only a preliminary review of the literature is usually required because there is an expectation that further work will be done on this during the course of study. However, the review included should demonstrate that you are conversant with the appropriate range of literature, particularly key and recent publications that pertain to your proposed topic. These serve to indicate that you have some basic skills of information retrieval and organisation that contribute to a justification for a developing topic focus.

For a proposal for *research funding* for a project beyond research degree level there are different requirements, whether the project is one of your own devising or one that is to fit in with the funders' own framework. You will be expected to be thoroughly conversant with the topic and others' views on it as expressed in the literature as this will demonstrate that you have expertise in the topic area and in information retrieval and organisation. Seldom will the literature review form a time-consuming part of and/or a key aspect of the research for which you are seeking financial support, unless the research is genuinely into a previously unexplored area that requires consideration of overlapping or cognate areas as they emerge during the process of exploration, or unless the focus of your project is the literature itself. More likely during the funded research project, you will simply be keeping up to date a literature base that you produced to formulate your proposal argument for funding.

The size of the review should reflect the degree of depth of exploration, not merely the number of references accessed. It will depend on the situation, whether seeking a *degree place* or *funding*, and the requirements of the proposal reviewer, but also on the proposed approach to the empirical work. At one extreme, for a project in a well-researched area seeking substantial funding to move the boundaries forward, a full, systematic literature review will be required to support the specific focus. This will take the form of a thorough search of the full literature using explicit eligibility criteria to identify studies with valid evidence, which are then rigorously appraised for their significance to the research topic. At the other extreme, if a **grounded theory** approach is taken (see the Glossary and the section entitled 'Research using interpretivist approaches' in Chapter 6), then the literature will be reviewed as it becomes relevant to emerging data and concepts so that the proposal requires an introduction and rationale but not a formal literature review. In between there can be a review that identifies a region within a topic area that appears to be under-researched, with a further review suggested to focus in greater depth as the project progresses.

Another key consideration when preparing the review is that this part of the proposal should demonstrate the insightfulness of your selection of book/articles to review. These documents should be demonstrably relevant to the purpose of your research, a statement of which can usefully form the starting point of your introduction or background description. (Most definitely it should not be taken as an opportunity to demonstrate how many books and articles you have read in the discipline.) This section should also frame the research by briefly describing the context of the present research, perhaps including the historical background to the general area and then locating the specific topic within the contemporary context, so that the relevant theoretical discourse can be identified. It follows from this that you should show how your study fits into a particular view of how science (meaning research in general, not the disciplines per se) should be conducted, what system of meanings it relates to and what assumptions are being made. This is sometimes called the research **paradigm**, or perspective taken, in the literature. We will discuss this in greater depth in Chapters 5 and 6 but note its relevance here because the pervading paradigm will influence what kind of questions are asked about the world. If the paradigm is stated early on, the reader can be orientated towards what to expect from the rest of the proposal so that false expectations are not raised.

Thus a brief indication of the body of literature that provides the context for your study will be sufficient because you must quickly, but with a transparent rationale, focus on the substantive theories and pertinent issues, the niche area in which your research lies. Within that it is important to identify the key authors, those who contributed to the historical development of ideas, the landmark studies that should be given credit, as well as those researchers/authors who are currently involved in the field, producing new theoretical insights. This process involves much reading through an analytical lens, noticing which studies and authors are most frequently referenced, which seem to be most representative of the area, as well as those that are influential and those that produce the most cogent arguments. It is important to remember not to neglect opponents as well as proponents of key interpretations (and overlaps with other bodies of literature) so that you can familiarise yourself thoroughly with the debates that pervade the subject.

THE PROCESS OF SEARCHING THE LITERATURE

Accessing this literature is a process of identifying appropriate key words and using them to search computerised databases in your field. Your librarian can advise you on this, and introduce you to academic search engines, but you need to be clear about your own conceptual framework first so that the more obvious words emerge and then synonyms and related concepts can be considered using a thesaurus. At first you may find a very large number of publications being generated by your first keyword/s so you will need to refine the search, perhaps by combining words/concepts (e.g. only A when it is with B). It is sensible only to seek out Abstracts at first, before trying to access the full publication, reviewing these to ensure that they do cover what the word search indicates – not all will, you will find. The experience, common to most researchers, of being occasionally disappointed that key words do not unlock insights into the topics you are interested in, emphasises the need to produce accurate Abstracts of your own work, a topic we will, apparently perversely, turn to in the final chapter.

You will discover too that a review is a process of progressive focussing, starting with a wide canvas but gradually honing in on those selected publications that best support your choice of topic and approach to it. A simple analogy captures the essence of this. If you look up the key word 'flowers' on your computer search engine you may, like us, get 144,000,000 references; if you add in 'nasturtiums', the result then is 85,200; next join in 'edibility' and the number of references is reduced to 26,000; follow this by adding 'UK vendors' and at last a more manageable figure of 9,370 references is produced. This is still a large number so if you do want to study this area then a further refinement of key words is needed, though if you scan this current list then you will already recognise that some sources are frequently repeated.

ACTIVITY 10 PRACTICE LITERATURE SEARCH

1 Just to get a feel for the task, access a computer and type into the web search engine the main descriptor of the realm you want to study. Note the number of sites found.
2 Then refine the descriptor in some sensible way and note the new number of sites.
3 Then refine the search by asking for scholarly journal articles on that topic.

(We tried 'doctoral education' – over 8.5 million sites; then added the scholarly articles refinement to reduce the number to about a quarter of a million . . .)

CONSTRUCTING YOUR ARGUMENT

Next, you must synthesise your own argument, drawing on your now refined literature set by reviewing in a critical manner the results presented and the methods used to produce them. Your argument should demonstrate clearly which issues have been robustly supported in the previous literature, and which issues are presented more tenuously or are controversial or even neglected, and therefore demand further investigation. You may find that there is a model that you can cite as your conceptual framework or one that requires development in the light of new evidence; you may be seeking to verify a theory or generate a new one so your literature review should not simply be a backward look at what previous research and writing has said to influence the focus of your research. It should also contain an element of prediction of how your research will contribute to the literature and what the results might add to the body of knowledge. Many research textbooks refer to 'identifying a gap' in the literature that your research is intended to bridge. This may be a phenomenon or method that is relatively unexplored or unexploited. All funders will expect some publication and dissemination of your work to materialise so acknowledge this fact in this section by showing the connections of your projected work to the existing literature, indicating what hole it will fill and which theories it seeks to substantiate, enhance, refine or confront.

A convincing argument can only be made through a logical presentation that is conceptually organised, with commonalities noted and comparisons made in some thematic way. If the review is extensive then sub-headings might be useful under which trends can be identified and limitations noted as you appraise previous work in the field. You must take care to acknowledge which ideas are your own and which you have derived from the work of others by careful referencing; similarly you should express all of this in your own words, only using quotations sparsely as illustration rather than substituting for your own formulation, so that you do not plagiarise the efforts of others. This is part of making the research project your own. Again, it is tempting to list a large number of other researchers or authors to give credibility to your argument, but it is wiser to demonstrate how conversant with the field you are by selecting the most significant of a list of potential references. If there are several important ones that support a point you are making then ensure that you are consistent in the way you present 'strings' of references. One convention is to list them in descending date order, that is, the most recent first, though some writers use alphabetic order of the first authors. Whichever convention you choose, stick with it in any one document.

Whilst engaged with isolating the most relevant topic during this process you should also note the methodological approaches, research designs and techniques used by significant players in the field, with a view to providing a similarly critical defence of your own selected approach and methods in the Methodology section (see Chapter 6).

In this chapter we have provided guidance on what you should do in relation to developing your ideas and providing a justification of choices made about what to study, and you may now be understanding more forcefully why we suggested at the beginning of this book that you should allow plenty of time for preparing a proposal. We can summarise the main points of this chapter differently by considering in Box 9 what a poor rationale/literature review would be like.

BOX 9 WHAT TO AVOID WHEN PRESENTING A REVIEW OF THE LITERATURE

- A poor review is unstructured, disorganised, verbose and repetitious.
- It lacks coherence, focus, critical evaluation and diligent acknowledgement and referencing.
- It neglects consideration of influential and current studies and relies on secondary sources.
- It thereby fails to identify appropriate research questions or hypotheses.

To evade these pitfalls, you might like, once you have produced a good draft of your literature section, to review it using the checklist in Box 10.

BOX 10 IMPORTANT ELEMENTS OF A LITERATURE REVIEW

Does your rationale/literature review section contain, in consistent format:

- an introduction explaining the purpose of the proposed research and how the review is organised to demonstrate that the purpose is worthwhile?
- headings (and sub-headings, if necessary) that tell the story in a logical order?
- signposts to guide the reader through the topics under discussion?
- selected references that represent the most recent and important contributions to the field?
- comparisons between and evaluation of the methods and results of the literature cited?
- clear links between the literature of the past and what you intend to do, showing why it is important and relevant?

Finally, your own rigorous version will then conclude by identifying not only relevant research questions or hypotheses but also ones that have the potential to form the basis of viable research practice, an issue we turn to in the following chapter.

ACTIVITY 11 LEARNING FROM THE LITERATURE REVIEWS OF OTHERS

This would be a good point at which to turn back to the successful proposals you identified in Activity 7 to focus on the literature review/rationale sections and analyse how they avoided the errors noted in Box 9 and conformed to the advice given in this chapter. You could also note any presentational aspects that you found helpful in navigating those reviews so that you could adapt them for your own writing.

REFLECTION POINT: CONTEMPLATING KEY FIGURES IN THE FIELD AND WHAT REMAINS TO BE STUDIED IN IT

Consider whether you can identify the main researchers/authors who have contributed to your chosen research area. Think about which ones are repeatedly cited.

Contemplate what the key outstanding areas are for further/future study.

5

WHAT IS THE SIGNIFICANCE OF THE AIMS, OBJECTIVES AND RESEARCH QUESTIONS/ HYPOTHESES?

CHAPTER OVERVIEW

This chapter discusses:

- choosing the level of specificity for aims and objectives;
- what these terms really mean;
- the essence of research questions and hypotheses;
- how they relate to theoretical assumptions and paradigms;
- the importance and impact of paradigm choice;
- the link between aims and research questions/hypotheses.

LEVEL OF SPECIFICITY REQUIRED

Whether you are seeking an opportunity to engage in doctoral study, or funding for that study or for a research project as an independent researcher, the refinement of your purpose for the research is one of the most difficult tasks in developing a research proposal. This critical stage involves describing the problems you intend to resolve, including the kind of answers sought, with an indication of how you expect to gain them. However, while for doctoral study there will be an opportunity to refine your ideas even further during the course of registration through further recourse to the literature and discussion with your supervisors/advisors, for independent research you will need to present much more detailed and specific aims and objectives which result in well-articulated research questions or hypotheses.

Most of this chapter will be devoted to aiding those of you who are in that latter category, but the discussion will be useful for future reference for those of you intent on pursuing doctoral-level study through a *research degree*. Your aims and objectives are likely to be couched at a more general level at this point, with the research questions/hypotheses less tightly focused. Indeed, some institutions, or departments within them, may be willing to accept a proposal to explore a certain dimension or theme within a sub-discipline area, or at a point of contact between discipline areas, without the specific topic being identified, as long as they have academic staff interested in it who would be willing to work with the proposer either to develop the proposal further or to refine the focus as part of the degree studies. Others may require you to demonstrate a more specific interest and to produce a more focussed proposal. Thus the advice provided here will be useful to you now or shortly.

These cases highlight another potential distinction between proposers. Some of you will be formulating a proposal autonomously – the choice of field and topic is entirely your own – while others are more constrained by a pre-defined problem space or theme, for instance those responding to a particular call for proposals:

- for contract research on a specified topic;
- to meet a strategic aim or research priority area of the funding organisation;
- to join a particular research team following a programme within a research area.

Whichever of these applies, you are likely to be expected (check audience requirement yet again) to formulate aims and objectives and the subsequent research questions/hypotheses in your own words, transforming the research problem identified through your literature review into something both transparent and researchable.

CLARIFICATION OF TERMS – AIMS AND OBJECTIVES

Let us clarify these terms at this point. The aims and objectives provide the terms of reference for your project, the aims stating the purpose or intent of the research. The aim derives from the problem/s noted in the literature review and may address a:

- disputed area (theoretical or philosophical) within the literature, seeking to resolve it;
- neglected area, seeking to identify characteristics and their relationships;
- topic previously accepted as understood but now identified as having flaws in logic or analysis, to rectify understanding;
- gap in knowledge, to bridge or fill the void;
- gap between an observed state and some preferred or normative state (for example, one that meets legal requirements or professional standards), to identify how a change from one to another might be effected.

The aim should ostensibly be feasible and also should take into account any specialist knowledge and/or skill and/or available opportunity (such as access to a particular data source) that you, the researcher, has, in order to reach the defined solution or answer to the research problem. Most importantly, the aim should focus on a research problem that is worthwhile addressing. As we said previously, there are many 'interesting' questions but the focus for any proposal that requires the use of scarce resources (including your time) should be constructive and productive. In particular, during a period of austerity in the UK at the time of writing, research councils and other funders want to be convinced of the potential of the research to make a 'significant impact' of some kind before they will part with money.

Objectives specify outcomes that contribute to and are necessary for the attainment of the aim. These outcomes need to be specific (precise), clearly defined (identifiable) and tangible (observable and preferably measurable in some way). These objectives do not have to specify how they will be met, for that is the task of the research design (see the next chapter), but it is important to be able to recognise when each objective has been met. Producing such specific objectives in relation to a clearly articulated aim, framed within the body of existing knowledge, takes time but helps to ensure that the scope of the research questions or hypotheses is limited to what is practically achievable. They will help to frame what can and cannot be tackled in the time frame allowed and the resources available, and what must be excluded from consideration for this project at this time.

This is a very important step because the contrast to clear aims with defined objectives with recognisable outcomes leading to answerable questions or testable hypotheses is, sadly, woolly aims with unachievable objectives (or objectives whose outcome is difficult to identify) leading to unanswerable questions or untestable hypotheses (See the example in Box 11). Similarly, a grandiose aim will result in so many objectives that the time and resources available are bound to be insufficient. This focus on what is achievable must go hand in hand with explicit, transparent meaning.

BOX 11 THE RAMIFICATIONS OF A WOOLLY AIM: AN EXAMPLE

Many researchers are tempted 'to investigate the effectiveness of a certain practice' (at work, in sport or the arts, and so forth) and some set off immediately to **survey** practitioners and their clients, only to discover that 'effectiveness', like beauty, is in the eye of the beholder.

It is also experienced differently according to context and previous experience and is thus subject to a range of definitions and criteria.

Similarly, what constitutes the 'practice' may differ between practitioners or be implemented differently by the same practitioner on different occasions or in varied contexts.

If a survey uses both of these terms, each of which lacks definition, then the results would be discounted as nonsense.

RESEARCH QUESTIONS AND HYPOTHESES

Thus the goal of preparing research questions or hypotheses is to attain clarity, with terms either defined unambiguously or their meaning specifically explored within the research. Research questions or hypotheses should also indicate what kind of data will be required to answer or confirm/refute them. Additionally, although any research project might provide descriptions of who, what, when and where, a contribution to knowledge generally requires an analytic approach to data that will answer the why and how questions.

PARADIGMS

We need to define a specific term here before we consider the next stage of the process, that is, the development of research questions or hypotheses. The term is 'paradigm'. This concept will be explored further in the next chapter on methodology but for now suffice it to say that a *paradigm* is a basic set of beliefs and assumptions, a world view that underpins the theories and methodology of a subject and thus guides action. The ultimate truthfulness of any paradigm can never be established and hence there are several competing ones; however, the strength of paradigms lies in their consistency and explanatory power. The constituents of any paradigm are its theories about the nature of reality – the nature of knowledge and how knowledge can be acquired. Therefore the paradigm espoused by an individual or group will determine what is deemed as relevant information and hence what questions are asked. The main paradigms in common currency in research today are positivism, post-positivism, **constructivism** and critical theory.

Research encompassed by the first two has a **nomothetic** aim, that is, relating to the generation of laws or at least generalisations. It tends to focus on investigating and explaining the relationships between phenomena, which may be causal or correlated, and involves determination and **manipulation of variables** involved in a situation. Researchers using this frame of reference deduce possible explanations, refine them and then propose an explanation in the form of a **hypothesis**, that is, a statement about a measurable relationship between two or more variables. Thus the data collected tend to be quantitative in nature, and these paradigms are the dominant ones (but not the only ones) in the natural and life sciences.

On the other hand, rather than explaining how things relate to each other, the research in the last two cases (constructivism and critical theory) is focussed on understanding the world from the point of view of the individual or groups of people interacting in and with it. Rather than seeking objective measurement in a reductionist format, as in the first two cases, the objective is to recognise the value-laden nature of interpretations, whether they are interpretations of an object, situation or activity. The philosophy underpinning this perspective is that the complexity and interconnectedness of any natural system demands a (w)holistic approach because not all variables can be identified while manipulating those that are unethical or would destroy the nature of the system. Thus research questions rather than hypotheses are pursued, the data are more frequently but not exclusively qualitative, while these approaches to research are most often found in the social sciences and in the arts and humanities.

WHY PARADIGM IDENTIFICATION IS IMPORTANT

The importance and impact of paradigm choice and its applicability in different circumstances can be best illustrated by an example. Suppose, for instance, that a potential researcher identifies in the context of his/her professional practice (C) some procedure (Z) that has been criticised as unproductive, and then comes across in a professional publication some descriptions of a new procedure (innovation X) which, when applied in other similar but not identical contexts, occasionally produced observable improvements in productivity. The research issue is whether or not an improvement might be obtained by implementing this new approach, innovation X, instead of procedure Z in context C relevant to the researcher. If the researcher espoused a positivist philosophy, an aim akin to the following might be devised: 'to compare the productivity in context C when the innovation X is implemented and when normal procedure Z is used'. Alternatively, if the researcher were of a constructivist orientation, the aim of a project might be 'to analyse the potential benefit of innovation X, in specific context C, and to identify factors that will influence its replacement of procedure Z and its implementation'. Because the aims are different so too will be the objectives, the positivist researcher seeking to measure productivity in the normal and in the experimental situation while the constructivist researcher is looking for information on benefits and limitations and factors that may influence them.

ACTIVITY 12 FACTORS THAT INFLUENCE PARADIGM CHOICE

Before reading on, consider the different contexts that this scenario might describe:

- Case A: The researcher might be a scientist in a laboratory (C) engaged in growing organisms with some little success in a particular medium (Z) who comes across an article about similar organisms being grown with some greater success in medium X.
- Case B: The researcher might be a manager in a factory (C) engaged in producing widgets with some little success through a particular process (Z) who comes across an article about similar widgets being produced with some greater success using process X.
- Case C: The researcher might be a teacher in a classroom (C) engaged in teaching children reading with some little success using approach (Z) who comes across an article about similar pupils being taught reading with some greater success using approach X.

Think about the different factors that will come into play in each scenario, and how those factors might influence which paradigm is chosen and hence which aims might be adopted in each case. Try to do this before you read further.

Some of the factors that you might have considered in the preceding activity could have included:

- The practical ease of changing from Z to X – would such a change involve very different materials, equipment, skills or experience? How readily are these obtained?
- The nature of context C – is it simple or complex, fixed or variable, controlled or uncontrollable?
- Political issues – would and should the organisms/workers/children have a say about the changeover and if so how might that influence the process?
- Ethical issues – is the change likely to cause harm? Are individuals' rights protected?

For Case A the change of medium might be relatively easy, the laboratory conditions may be simple and fixed or readily controlled, and the organisms have no say in the matter and are not considered as having rights, so an experimental approach could be employed that derives from a hypothesis such as:

> A greater number of organisms will grow in a fixed time period and in standardised laboratory conditions on medium Z than on medium X.

For Case B, if the practical changes are readily implementable, at least on a small scale, if the context is relatively simple and if the workers and their unions are amenable to undertaking the change because no harm is likely to ensue (no redundancies, for instance), then again a hypothesis might be devised, and an experiment implemented, such as:

> Workers using process X will produce more widgets than those using process Z over a specified period of time and in similar factory conditions.

However, if the changes involve either more expensive equipment, and/or considerable training, and/or might raise the spectre of redundancies and/or involve the workers in potentially harmful procedures, then a research question such as the following might be derived:

> What are the potential benefits and limitations of the change from Z to X from the point of view of the different stakeholders?

For Case C, again consideration will need to be given to the practical consequences of change, the complexity of the environment and the **participants**, and the views of other stakeholders such as the director of education and the school inspectors, not to mention the parents of the pupils; but predominantly there would be the ethical problem of experimenting on children and potentially causing some children to do less well at reading than others.

If an experiment would be considered at all, it would need to address these complexities, perhaps through first gaining permissions from all relevant stakeholders for the implementation of a careful design using a Reading Test K that identifies the number of words identified correctly over a specified reading time to test a hypothesis such as:

> When a stratified **sample** of pupils are taught using approach X for (specified period) and tested before and after using standardised Reading Test K and then taught for the same period using approach Z, again tested employing the same test, and when a similar stratified sample are taught using approach Z and then approach X, and tested on the three occasions – before, midway and after using the same test – then the reading gains (number of words correctly identified) will be greater after each of the periods using the approach X.

Alternatively, instead, the researcher may take another perspective altogether, though still needing to acquire the relevant permissions, perhaps considering that the individual's experience of learning to read is more important than the number of words identified in a specific time, and so may pose the research questions:

> How do pupils respond in relation to their experience of learning to read after a fixed period using approach X and after the same period using approach Z? What other differences between pupils might influence their experience of each approach?

From the above, three particularly important points emerge:

1 Different contexts and discipline areas, and combinations of the two, lend themselves to different possibilities and paradigms for research.
2 Approaches derived from different paradigms lead either to questions or hypotheses.
3 Research hypotheses and questions imply different research activities and different data sets.

We will pursue the implications in (3) in the next chapter but, before we leave the technicalities of research hypotheses and questions, some consideration is required of how they derive from objectives, particularly in relation to how clearly and specifically they are expressed.

THE LINK BETWEEN AIMS/OBJECTIVES AND RESEARCH QUESTIONS/HYPOTHESES

It is likely that aims and objectives viewed from within a constructivist or critical theory perspective will produce an overarching research question, derived from the aim, and a set of sub-questions which result from the list of objectives, which may be numerous in a complex situation. Please note that all of the resulting sub-questions should be clear, unambiguous and researchable – that is, we should be able to see that data can be found which will contribute to the formulation of an answer. They should also be interconnected so that ultimately the combined answers contribute to a response to, or resolution of, the research problem. They often take the form of 'what is happening?' and 'how?'.

If now we turn to the case of preparing hypotheses, as required by positivist research approaches, we find that there is a parallel requirement for clarity and specificity. Indeed there is a technical term for turning informal hypotheses, or 'intuitive theories', into research hypotheses. The term 'operationalising' the hypothesis gives us a clue that the process is intended to make the problem one that is open to practical testing. Further, by operationalising the hypothesis the researcher establishes principles and assumptions that orientate the research – for instance:

- what the target population is (e.g. in social sciences or humanities) or what the research objects are (e.g. in arts or sciences);
- what boundaries of space and time confine the research;
- what variables, and in what form, might influence results.

Each hypothesis should be predictive about a relationship between two or more variables and should be written in a form that allows it to be tested. This means that key variables need to be clearly identified, the context defined and the outcomes measurable (e.g. specified organisms in specified conditions and a specified way of measuring growth, or specified processes, with specific kinds of widgets, and a measurable production rate, and so forth). However, a hypothesis is by nature a speculation and so it is usual to produce a **null hypothesis** (the research hypothesis in negative form) to allow for the possibility of refutation of the research hypothesis. This usually takes the form that the speculated relationship between variables does not exist. The results of the research experiment should then allow either the hypothesis or the null hypothesis to be rejected.

Before proceeding with considering how you will conduct your research and describe it in your proposal, ensure that you are familiar with the criteria for generating either research questions or hypotheses. Appendix 2 lists some textbooks you might find useful in clarifying your understanding. You may be ready to formulate your questions or hypotheses now or you may wish to reserve that task until after working through the next chapter, which considers the range of possible research designs and methods and how these are required to be presented in a research proposal.

REFLECTION POINT: MOVING FROM AIMS TO DATA THROUGH YOUR APPROACH

Consider your aims and objectives – will these readily convert into research questions or hypotheses? What kind of data are likely to contribute to resolving the research problem you have identified? What paradigm or general research approach is indicated?

6

WHAT SHOULD BE INCLUDED IN THE METHODOLOGY/RESEARCH IMPLEMENTATION SECTIONS?

CHAPTER OVERVIEW

This chapter discusses:

- maintaining consistency across purpose, design and implementation;
- shorthand terms used to describe research;
- the depth of methodology description required in different circumstances;
- demonstrating a logical, coherent plan;
- positivist research to produce quantitative data and modes of analysis;
- interpretivist research to produce mainly qualitative data and modes of analysis;
- the salience of using the right language;
- the importance of ethical considerations;
- planning for evaluation as part of your project.

CONSISTENCY BETWEEN PURPOSE AND PROCEDURES

The discussion about paradigms in the previous chapter reminds us that, in addition to research proposals requiring a significant and analytical literature review to justify the research problem to be addressed and the theoretical approach to be taken, there is also the burden of explaining and defending the choice of research approach/philosophy, consequent research design and then selection of research instruments and techniques. There should be a transparent and obvious **correlation** between the approach and design/instruments/techniques so that they make sense as a system within a particular paradigm. The description and justification of that system is generally termed the **methodology** (usually a proposal section in its own right) and this is followed by or includes a description of the planned research implementation (laboratory, fieldwork, documentary analysis or creative art, and so forth). Again the task of the proposal producer is to present a logical argument supported by evidence, this time about the intended process of the research rather than the intended final product of the research, although the interim product of raw data will be a critical aspect of this section.

CLARIFICATION OF 'SHORTHAND' TERMS

Before addressing the detail of the content of this section it is worthwhile discussing a common misunderstanding – or rather mis-attribution – that arises when workers within disciplines or sub-disciplines use abbreviations or words that are well understood in that system. One case is the term 'data' that pervades the sciences and social sciences as a term to denote pieces of information. We hope that colleagues in the arts and humanities who prefer other terms will tolerate the use of data in this text. Another example is the use of the adjectives 'quantitative' and 'qualitative'. Not only do textbooks abound with the terms 'qualitative research' or 'quantitative research' in the titles, but in addition, the majority of methods books use the terms as a shorthand for describing research methods producing data that are non-numerical or numerical in nature. Because such data are more usually found in work following, respectively, the constructivist/critical theory approaches or positivist approaches, this then leads to erroneous assumptions that if the researcher is to be consistent within an approach, mixed methods would be problematic.

This is an example of taking assumptions one step too far because, although data can be either qualitative or quantitative, any approach can use either or both kinds of data to resolve problems. In order to avoid any problems in the discussion that follows we will refer to positivist and interpretivist approaches as our shorthand terms and we will assume which data which are either qualitative or quantitative in nature might be sought to resolve problems.

METHODOLOGY – APPROACH AND JUSTIFICATION

For those of you who are seeking to embark on the formal study of research as well as to put your learning into practice through an engagement with a project that is the basis of a *research degree* programme, any commitment to a particular philosophical research position prior to registration may be premature because exploration of contrasting positions often forms a significant part of research methods training in most institutions, at least in Europe. However, particularly in the social sciences and to some extent in the life sciences, particular research groups favour one approach over another and thus will look more enthusiastically at proposals which raise issues that would respond to investigations using their preferred approach and methods. Therefore another reason for exploring potential doctoral course providers is to seek indications of preferred methodologies in relation to expertise in sub-discipline areas (see the section below entitled 'Using the right language' for clues on how to recognise proponents of a particular philosophy from their writing). This should be done in order to orientate your proposal accordingly rather than to reject the possibility of engaging in a research approach with which you may not yet be familiar. It could be that you will relish the new perspectives that a different approach could bring. On the other hand, it would be foolish to select as potential supervisors people who apparently view the world of research from a very different perspective than you do.

While you may not need to engage in depth with the brief foray into philosophy that follows, you should certainly be able to speculate in your proposal about what kind of design and methods and techniques could be useful in your proposed research to demonstrate that you know something about the practice of research. If you present some suggestions you can also indicate that these will be subject to further review over the initial period of study, and do not preclude alternatives. What is more, you may find the discussion interesting and perhaps it will be useful to help you show erudition in any selection interviews you may be invited to attend. (For those for whom methodology is relatively unfamiliar territory, a Glossary of key terms used here is provided at the end of the book. It also contains brief explanations of other technical words commonly used in other sections of a proposal, for example in the budget section.)

Conversely, those submitting proposals for *funding* for post-doctoral or other non-degree research will be expected to be conversant with research approaches and methods and be able to justify their choice of paradigm or philosophical approach. In the natural sciences this tends to be unproblematic, for the nature of problems usually demands a research hypothesis which can be tested using an experimental or quasi-experimental approach, either of which are a neat fit in the positivist or neo-positivist paradigm. In other disciplines the decision may be less clear cut and will depend on the researcher's theory about:

- what the nature of reality is (**ontology**);
- what knowledge is (**epistemology**);
- how knowledge can be gained (methodology).

These are clearly not trivial differences in perspective, for a belief that:

> reality is objective, singular and apart from/uninfluenced by the researcher who can investigate it in a value- and bias-free (positivistic) way

is at odds with a belief that:

> reality is subjective and multiple as it is interacted with by participants in the study, including the researchers, who in turn have to recognise and declare their inevitably value-laden and biased (interpretivist) approach.

CONSISTENCY AND JUSTIFICATION

Because this is not a research methodology textbook (see Appendix 2 for some suggestions about useful research methodology textbooks) there is no space to go into great detail about these important debates between adherents of alternative paradigms, fascinating though these are; but it is critical in a proposal that the research design, data-collecting methods, instruments and analysis techniques are internally consistent, relevant and appropriate to the research question or hypothesis. A rationale for the choice of general approach and then for the selection of design, and so on, within it should be presented with support from the literature on research practice and with reference to the literature describing and evaluating previous research in the area. An important point to remember is that the term 'rationale' means more than simply providing the beneficial or good aspects of something; it also incorporates acknowledging its limitations, along with suggestions about how their impact can be effectively reduced, as well as providing reasons why other potential alternatives were rejected .... So your rationale must be a carefully honed argument.

As we indicated in the previous chapter, any rationale for the process of the research project should also be intimately linked to the purpose of the research. If the aim is to produce and quantify similarities and differences, to produce comparisons in standardised forms, or to determine measurable relationships between variables, then the strategies to produce deductions from pertinent and viable data will be different from those used to meet the aim of understanding meanings or interpretations of things or processes and how those meanings/interpretations interact through an inductive process.

Whichever of these is the case for you, the design for any kind of project is a procedural plan. Box 12 summarises what should be encompassed within the research design for a social science or science project. There is likely to be less emphasis in the arts and humanities on equipment, instruments and measuring scales, for example, but the order and type of work with a rationale will be required nonetheless.

BOX 12 THE ELEMENTS OF A RESEARCH DESIGN

The design section of a proposal should:

- express the logic that underpins the planned strategy;
- include details of the procedures involved including any equipment or instruments used;
- describe how different parts of the process interrelate;
- define the characteristics of the research population;
- provide the particulars about numbers and types of samples;
- anticipate problems and posit potential solutions;
- describe and justify the measuring scales, data analysis and interpretation methods;
- convey familiarity with and confidence in handling the procedures, equipment and instruments.

RESEARCH USING POSITIVIST APPROACHES

A positivist strategy must include within its design (to study cause and effect or correlation) a pre-determination of measurable variables some of which will be manipulated (**independent variables**) while the effect on others (**dependent variables**) is observed. Yet other variables are held constant or assumed to vary randomly. Special care must be taken to identify **confounding variables** – those that will particularly distort the results if not controlled (and those that reviewers are sure to worry about if you fail to mention them). The design that is considered the gold standard in clinical contexts is the randomised controlled trial (RCT) – a study in which people are allocated at random to receive one of several clinical interventions. One of these interventions is the standard of comparison or control. The control may be a standard practice, a placebo or no intervention at all, against which the intervention being tested is measured. Another frequently used design, termed 'pre-test post-test', involves measurement of a phenomenon before and after an intervention.

PRESENTING AND ANALYSING QUANTITATIVE RESULTS

The data are likely to include information that can be presented as **descriptive statistics** but the results of interventions or experiments need also to be subjected to statistical analysis to determine if any effects could occur by chance or are likely, at a certain pre-set **confidence level**, to be a result of the experimental manipulation. Again the choice of inferential statistical tests used needs to be defended because they each require that the data fit particular parameters – if your project is in any way complex it is no bad thing to indicate that you will employ the services of an expert statistician (assuming you are not one yourself) but remember to account for this when preparing your budget (Chapter 7). Sometimes newer researchers reject positivist hypothesising because they fear the rigour involved alongside having to engage with complex calculations using statistics. It is important to recognise that there are equal but different rigours inherent in collecting qualitative data which itself involves complicated analytical procedures. It is more important to feel philosophically at ease with the concepts entailed in an approach than to let numbers or complicated procedures be the stumbling block to the appropriate choice.

The concepts of **validity** and **reliability** are important parameters of measurement in positivist research, each having sub-categories that demand address in the rationale for the study to demonstrate that the data are appropriate to the research purpose and the techniques to gather it do so in a consistent and unadulterated manner. In situations such as those involving human subjects in which it is difficult, practically or ethically, to manipulate or control all variables then the design needs to accommodate that. This is often achieved by randomly allocating subjects to control and **experimental groups**, as in the RCT described above. All of this is important to produce context-free results which can lead to generalisations.

ACTIVITY 13 DEFINING CONCEPTS FOR POSITIVIST RESEARCH

Before going further, look at the indicative (but certainly not exhaustive) list of key concepts below and try to formulate a definition or description of them so that you can demonstrate understanding of them in your proposal, whether you intend to subscribe to them or reject them. You can check your answers in the Glossary and then go on to elaborate your understanding by reference to a good methodology book such as those listed in Appendix 2.

CONCEPT LIST RELEVANT FOR POSITIVIST RESEARCH

Independent variable	Dependent variable
Confounding variable	Control group
Descriptive Statistics	Inferential statistics
Validity	Reliability
Nomothetic	Reductionist
Confidence level	Generalisable result

RESEARCH USING INTERPRETIVIST APPROACHES

Different concepts from those described above are considered important in interpretive research because there is the fundamental assumption that individual participants will hold different world views while their very engagement in the research might well impact on those views. Thus a concern for validity is replaced by a search for **authenticity**, the recognition of appropriateness to the participants and to the context – place and time. Reliability is not expected because the researcher, with participants, shapes the emerging factors but, as in the positivist approach, accuracy is sought, this time through verification by participants and/or by **triangulation** of methods so that data from one perspective (for example, from a technique such as interview) are compared with data from one or more other methods (say, from **observation** and questionnaire). Utility to the participants is also an important aspect because the exploration of meaning must be of some value to them if they are to engage effectively with the process. The design is often an emerging one with successive explorations following one from another, in an iterative pattern, while the data frequently take the form of categories identified during the research process. This last point is important because the pre-formation of categories by the researcher could be said to contradict the espoused intent of seeking the meaning of others.

There are many variants within the family of interpretivist research from overarching approaches such as **phenomenology** and **ethnomethodology**, through particular perspectives such as personal constructivism (a psychological orientation), social constructionism (a sociological orientation), narrative enquiry or feminism, to particular 'sensibilities' such as modern or postmodern. Because each brings with it a history, a set of assumptions, traditions and preferences in terms of method and the form that its data take, it is wise to clarify for the reviewer the particular stance taken and the implications it brings with it. Designs within this philosophy are varied, ranging from a grounded theory approach that makes no a priori assumptions, deriving theory from the data rather than from previous literature, through to explorations using data sets from many participants, to case studies of individuals. Each has its own strengths and limitations that should be discussed in the proposal along with, as in the positivist case above, anticipation of the unexpected with potential ploys to minimise its impact or take advantage of the new avenues it opens up.

There are many techniques or data collection methods associated with these interpretative approaches, such as interview, observation, **repertory grid**, document analysis, questionnaire and methods, that involve imagery or artefacts to elicit constructs about the world. They can be used individually or in combination (see triangulation above) but they each require a careful description about how they will be applied and what kind of data they are intended to produce. For instance, an interview might be very formally structured with set questions in fixed order with a supplied choice of potential answers, in which case the data could be quantitative in nature in a similar way to the data from a survey which has closed questions. On the other hand, the general topic might be pre-decided but the questions might be open ended and unstructured, building on and developing the answers to previous questions, and thus the order too would be fluid. This format would result in qualitative data. Thus the notion of a mixed or multi-method project emerges, the design of which could incorporate, for example, an initial survey collecting quantitative data from which particular individual participants might be identified for follow-up using semi-structured or unstructured interviews producing qualitative data for a more in-depth view. In contrast, the constructs (qualitative data) from repertory grids (a technique used in constructivist research) on a topic from a representative group – a small number of participants – might be used to provide the questions for a questionnaire that collects quantitative data from a large **population**. This ensures that the questions are couched in the language of the participant population and address concerns that are deemed somewhat more relevant to the population than those produced solely by researchers, from their inevitably different frame of reference.

Thus the researcher might use the data from one section of the project to inform and contribute to another section, in an iterative fashion.

PRESENTING AND ANALYSING QUALITATIVE RESULTS

The analysis of data in interpretivist approaches is complex because the data are itself complicated. Although descriptive statistics might be used to describe the more stable features of a range of participants (age, gender, profession, geographical location, for instance), the data they provide in answer to the research question are individual in nature and are likely to be in the form of voluminous extended text. Thus data management becomes a particularly significant part of the research design because a systematic, consistent and organised procedure is required for their collection, storage and retrieval. In order to avoid being overwhelmed by the data, a way of displaying them in various summarised forms (data reduction) should be devised in advance, and from this process, tactics for discerning patterns or themes and categories can be decided. This may involve coding the data in one form or another and often demands iteration, a recursive process of modification and refinement of the coding, themes and/or categories to uncover regularities. This is an inductive, rather than deductive, process and should be made transparent in the proposal. Reviewers will be conscious of the wealth of data that is likely to be elicited using these techniques and will need reassuring that the researcher will not drown in it but will be able to deal competently with it to produce an **audit trail** from raw data to final interpretations.

These interpretations should provide what is termed in some approaches a '**thick description**', one that provides understanding of a previously little-understood phenomenon within a particular context. Although generalisation is not sought in these approaches, because their purpose is to explore a particular case or cases, they can provide clues to aid sense-making in other similar cases/contexts, and this is known as **transferability** – the degree to which results from one study context could inform understanding of another, or at least provide some specific areas for exploration. However, their objective is primarily to be idiographic, to convey an understanding of the meanings of a situation, object and so forth from the perspectives of those involved rather than from that of the researcher.

ACTIVITY 14 DEFINING CONCEPTS FOR INTERPRETIVIST RESEARCH

Again, before going further, it is timely to check your understanding of terms. As in the previous activity, try to define the terms presented below, then check them with the Glossary and explore them further using a methodology textbook.

CONCEPT LIST RELEVANT FOR INTERPRETIVIST APPROACHES

Authenticity/credibility	Idiographic
Utility	Iterative design
Ethnomethodology	Phenomenology
Open questions	Unstructured interview
Mixed-method research	Transferability
Dependability	Confirmability

There are two more salient aspects to include in the methodology section of the proposal, regardless of its orientation. These are ethical considerations and a plan by which the research process can be evaluated. These are addressed below after a note about the key concerns, and the language used to express them, of proponents of different research paradigms.

USING THE RIGHT LANGUAGE

The issue of language use is often a key concern for adherents of the interpretivist approaches because meaning is often reflected in word choice and order, and it can be seen from the foregoing that the language used in each of the main paradigms we have discussed differs. For instance, positivists are concerned with the validity and reliability of their research as well as the objectivity with which it is conducted. For interpretivists, what is more important is the authenticity of the data they collect in terms of its credibility to the participant population. In addition, although they may expect individual respondents to develop their ideas during the course of the research, and probably to respond slightly differently in different contexts, so that reliability is not an issue, they nevertheless seek **dependability** – that those respondents would ratify any summary of their responses. You may have noticed too that, although adherents of both sorts of paradigms would recognise the term 'respondent', the positivists generally refer to the other people involved in the research as 'subjects' whereas interpretivists call them 'participants'. In some cases, for instance in **action research**, the researcher either is also a full participant or has only a facilitating role to the participants who bring the research problem to the fore and work together on its resolution. This reflects the contrasting ways in which control of the research is viewed by different researchers.

Thus the terminology and voice used in describing the research tends to mirror the paradigm in being objective and impersonal in the positivist framework while in interpretivist reports and descriptions the personal is acknowledged and even deliberately included to provide the frame of reference for data analysis and interpretations. **Confirmability** (ability to be corroborated) is more important in the latter case in contrast to the aim of objectivity in the first case. Thus, in developing your project proposal, being careful with language use, particularly concepts alluded to, is important for demonstrating familiarity with a paradigm and consistency of approach within it. Whether objectivity or acknowledgement of inevitable personal viewpoints orientates the project, a key concern is maintaining an ethical stance.

ETHICAL CONSIDERATIONS

In research, the term **ethics**, derived from the philosophical study of moral principles, is used to denote the code of conduct that determines how the research will be carried out. However, what actually constitutes ethical behaviour in research is socially and culturally defined, so that what was considered reasonable practice in the past, or in another context may not now or in your current context be deemed appropriate behaviour for a researcher. (For instance, in the past, psychological experiments in which subjects were misled about the purpose of what they were asked to engage in were normal practice but this approach has since been rejected, such deception now contravening the professional research code, which requires honesty.) While designing your research project it is important to find out about the particular stance and requirements of any funding body likely to be involved as well as any professional body requirements that might apply.

Many professional bodies have their own version of a code of ethics. These provide guidance when decisions about one form of action or another have to be made so that the choice is guided by principles rather than expediency, the latter being what is advantageous to the researcher or the completion of the research project. The principles focus on what is right and just for all those involved in the research or with its outcomes (participants, sponsors, subsequent users of the research products). Thus, even though your research may involve no living participants (human or animal), care has to be taken to consider the well-being of anyone who might be affected as a consequence of results being published or the work becoming part of the public domain in any way – ethics are a consideration for natural scientists and those working with documents as much as they are for social scientists or health scientists working with people in their research.

Protection of the safety of human subjects or participants should be of paramount concern, as should be respectful, humane and equitable treatment of them, whoever they are. One particular standard is the requirement for voluntary, **informed consent** to take part in research. In short, this means that the researcher should be honest about the nature of the research with people who are treated equally as fellow human beings, not as objects, and who understand the commitment and likely problems of being engaged in the research before agreeing to take part. The researcher should be intent on avoiding harm as well as intending to be morally good! It is important to gain informed consent and to keep rigorous records that indicate that you have done so. Part of those records should be an information sheet that includes an explanation of the research, or a summary of it if a verbal one is also provided, and a signed consent form that notes that:

- the signatory has received and read the information sheet or has had it read or explained to them;
- the purpose and structure of the project and what his/her part in it has been explained and agreed with;
- any questions have been answered to the satisfaction of the signatory;
- the signatory understands that participation is voluntary and that s/he may withdraw at any time with no detriment;
- authority is given to consult a particular professional if required (for example, their General Practitioner);
- a copy of the consent form has been received.

Obviously, special procedures apply in cases where informed consent cannot readily be obtained, for instance from children or people with difficulties in understanding, so advice should be sought from expert colleagues. Further, each subject/participant should be assured of anonymity to anyone other than the researcher/s, and this has implications for secure storage of anonymised and coded data separate from lists of participant details. Moreover, the data they provide should be considered confidential, that is, particular pieces of information should not be attributable to a particular identifiable person. This requires attention to storage as well as to collection and is part of the appropriate **curation** of data required by research funders. You should check on the specific ethical requirements related to your own research, perhaps undertaken in a particular professional context and funded by a defined sponsor. Either or both of these may require that you submit your plans to one or more ethics committee(s) (perhaps a university ethics committee and a regional health ethics committee, each of whom will work to their own code of ethical practice). Bear in mind that these committees are there not just to protect the rights of the general public but also the rights and reputations of researchers. You can see in Box 13 the scope of one university ethics committee that is similar to most.

BOX 13 THE SCOPE OF AN EXAMPLE UNIVERSITY ETHICS COMMITTEE

a Precise definitions are not possible but the following areas of research come within the terms of reference of the committee:

i those involving procedures of an invasive kind, e.g. the taking of tissue samples, the administration of substances or other medical or quasi-medical procedures;
ii testing procedures such as food acceptability trials, taste panels and so forth;
iii psychological, social science or humanities research involving human participants, including questionnaires, surveys, focus groups and other interview techniques;
iv educational research;
v research involving human data or records. Ethical concerns are strongest where these data are gathered directly from the subject and then ethical approval is usually required. Where the records are in the public domain, or where the subject is deceased, ethical considerations may still be relevant but such research does not normally require ethical approval;
vi research using personal information or samples stored from previous research (either initially or when a proposal is revised);
vii the use of biological samples that are anonymised or that consist of surplus tissue from routine operations.

b Investigators should be aware that any research which constitutes, or could be interpreted as constituting, an encroachment on personal privacy requires careful ethical consideration.
c Investigators must be aware of the Human Tissue Act 2004 and the Mental Capacity Act 2005. Further information on both these Acts and their implications for research ethics issues can be found on [the University Home Page].
d The Committee is happy to consider the ethical dimensions of projects which, while they may not come within a strict interpretation of the terms of reference, raise issues or use material of a kind which may be viewed with scepticism in a non-academic context.

Source: University of Reading

You can see that the range of projects that come under the remit of such committees is wide and that they are willing to provide advice in circumstances of uncertainty. However, you should prepare your proposal carefully and in good time for presentation to the ethics committee because they frequently meet only on particular dates, and the whole process can be time consuming, especially if your proposal is rejected and has to be re-submitted after specified amendments have been made. Thankfully, such committees are composed of those with research expertise and so can often provide extremely helpful feedback. However, it is best not to waste their time with poorly considered proposals. The next activity may help you avoid the more common pitfalls if your research involves human subjects/participants, human samples or human personal data relating to living people that is not in the public domain.

ACTIVITY 15 CHECKING YOUR RESEARCH DESIGN AGAINST ETHICAL CRITERIA

Interrogate your research design using the following questions, bearing in mind that, to be acceptable to any ethics committee, your responses should demonstrate that you have evaluated the risks of harm to any stakeholders and have sought to treat them with respect.

Does your research project:

1 cover any sensitive areas that may cause embarrassment, stress, anxiety or similar harmful emotional responses?
2 involve any activities that might be physically demanding?
3 put the subject/participant in a situation that might involve loss of self-esteem?
4 incorporate any burdensome commitment by the participant/subject that would disrupt their normal life?
5 require the engagement of particularly vulnerable individuals who may need special support or consideration?
6 impinge on anyone's right to privacy?
7 involve access to confidential data that require special attention to protection during storage and use?
8 have any element of risk (e.g. the taking of new medicinal drugs or engagement in extreme activity) that needs extra advice and time for more careful consideration by the participants?
9 avoid any hint of coercion to take part?

Will all your participants/subjects be:

1 informed about the nature and purpose of the research?
2 told how much time and effort will be required of them?

(Continued)

(Continued)

3 given information about steps taken to guard anonymity?
4 told about any potential intrusions or risks?
5 advised of any benefits of participation?
6 told that they can withdraw at any point at no disadvantage to themselves?
7 given contact details of a senior researcher who can respond to questions?
8 offered feedback on the study results?
9 asked to sign an informed consent form?

(These questions have been gathered from an analysis of a wide range of ethics committees' guidelines.)

EVALUATION PLAN

A final section in your proposal may be an evaluation plan. This is not always obligatory, though some funders may specify the kind of evaluation they expect you to engage in, from a simple question such as 'How will you know when you have achieved your objectives?' to a requirement for a detailed plan to measure that achievement in the form of a mini-research proposal. That plan should identify what results are required, how they will be measured and what evidence will support the achievement of those results. This should be followed by a description of how the data will be collected and analysed.

Beyond determining whether your specific objectives have been achieved, you may also need to reflect on the value of your results, the strength and limitations of your research process and appropriateness of methodology, and the direct and indirect benefits of the whole enterprise. (Incidentally, these same things should be included in the discussion section of a doctoral thesis.) One particularly salient concept at the time of writing (as noted earlier) is *impact*. This is the degree to which your research products (outputs/outcomes) will influence or have an effect on the specific audience for your research and/or wider society. Clearly, for funding organisations it is important that they will be provided with evidence that their investment was sound. Your evaluation should provide them with evidence about which of your objectives were achieved and what value for money they have gained. This will give them a baseline for the support of future similar research and, in your interest, it will indicate the potential value of extending your research. At a more basic level, an evaluation plan demonstrates your serious approach to providing quality research and that you are seeking ways to improve it.

There are benefits also to yourself and your own organisation in undertaking an evaluation of your research because it helps identify what is achievable and what is not within a certain time period with limited facilities and within budgetary constraints – the restrictions under which we all work. The results of the evaluation also provide extra grist to the mill for the dissemination of your work, providing substantiation of its quality.

Before we leave the topics of methodology and implementation to take up the challenge of developing a budget for your proposal, it is worth considering in the next activity what common faults reviewers will seek out in this section of a proposal.

ACTIVITY 16 CHECKING FOR PITFALLS IN RESEARCH DESIGN AND STRATEGY

Consider what you intend to include in your section on research design and strategy and how you will avoid the following pitfalls:

- unclear commitment to a general coherent research approach;
- lack of a well-thought-out rationale for the design and methods;
- vague action plan;
- lack of detail about research instruments and their strengths and weaknesses;
- limited or no discussion of relevant data analysis techniques;
- weak attention to ethical procedures;
- little thought given to evaluation of the project.

REFLECTION POINT: THE INTERACTION BETWEEN AIMS AND DESIGN

At this juncture you might like to consider whether your research question or hypothesis is such that you can provide a robust research design that uses your knowledge and skills, or whether you need to extend your knowledge and skills, or reconsider and refine your research aim.

7

WHAT FINANCIAL CONSIDERATIONS ARE REQUIRED?

CHAPTER OVERVIEW

This chapter discusses:

- the ground rules of budgeting for any research project;
- types and styles of budgets for different circumstances;
- key elements of budgets: personnel and operating costs;
- the budget post-proposal submission.

THE GROUND RULES OF BUDGETING

Obviously if you are seeking funding of any kind, either for supporting your studies at higher degree by research level or for an independent research project, budgets come strongly into the picture, but they are an important consideration too even if you are simply seeking an offer of a place to study for a doctorate. In this last case, your proposal should convince those academics assessing it that you have given serious thought to the financial viability of your proposed research. Further, programme administrators will also require evidence that you can support yourself through the programme if you do not have a maintenance grant, or stipend, as some funders refer to it. Thus, even if you are simply seeking a place to study for a research degree, you should find that reading this chapter helps with your immediate plans as well as giving you some insight into the workings of research budgets for the future.

THE FINANCIAL DEMANDS OF A RESEARCH DEGREE PROJECT

Nonetheless, for *research degree* proposals estimated costs only will suffice for specific requirements such as equipment, travel and subsistence (for data collection and dissemination activities such as conferences) and consumables (such as chemicals) or other vital experimental material. This speculation may still seem a daunting demand and one you may find difficult to fulfil. This is one of the very good reasons for making contact with a potential supervisor early in the process so that you can seek their advice about what is required, what will be supplied and what other potential financial sources of support exist from within and outside the institution. This will enable you to assess what you will ultimately be personally responsible for obtaining. If you are joining an established research group, or a project that has external funding obtained by the supervisor or Principal Investigator, it is likely that the main research equipment and materials will have been resourced already, but it will do no harm to indicate that you are cognisant that such things are costly and require effort to access. Even so, your specific part of a project may require time with expensive 'kit' (hardware of any kind, and also perhaps the use of specific software packages) that may be in high demand. Meanwhile, consumables for your own part of the project will need to be resourced.

Although costs for science projects are likely to be larger, arts, humanities and social science projects are not cost free, so if you are a non-scientist you should consider software requirements and also 'access costs', for example, fees for access to documents and/or travel to meet key information holders, as well as the traditional costs of books and stationery, photocopying and printing that are common to all projects. Some costs will be covered by your sponsor, if you have one – if not, then you should consider how you might support these costs from your personal resources or by seeking a small grant from a charity or trust fund (see Appendix 1). Remember that, although there may be some famous trust funds or charitable resources in your field, the competition for such funding is fierce and so it is best to consider it only for enhancing your research, not for the basic costs of pursuing your research. It is essential that you do not rely on winning extra funding for essential items from the institution or main funding agency once you have started. You should prepare in advance a range of options in your project plan so that your work does not grind to a halt because funding you hoped to get does not materialise.

Each university should be able to supply you with a guide to costs and their pricing policy – we cannot give you exact figures here because there are discipline/institutional/national differences and of course rates change with time and fiscal policy – but Table 2 provides some general guidance on what you should expect your sponsor to provide (but do check to be certain). Obviously if you are a self-funded student then you need to consider carefully how you might meet such costs.

TABLE 2 Guidance on pricing for research studentships

Cost	Pricing policy
Stipend or maintenance costs	Sponsors should cover these costs through a fixed rate per annum. It is worth checking any extra things that you can claim for, in addition to the main stipend. If you are self-funding, check out the going rate provided by national sponsors to give an indication of minimum levels required.
Composition/course fees	These are usually covered by the sponsor but in the UK the fees differ for home/EU and international students so check that your sponsor supports the full fee that you will be charged.
Consumables for research project (NB this is unlikely to include stationery items such as computer discs, paper, etc.)	Most sponsors cover this but they may set a maximum rate so careful planning is required to reduce waste to a minimum.
Funding for research training and conferences	Most sponsors provide financial support for essential research training and for some conference attendance but again most set a maximum rate per annum, which is likely to exclude overseas travel.
Overheads and bench fees	Most sponsors do not contribute to overhead costs and many, especially government-supported funders, do not pay bench fees but commercial sponsors should. These will be considerably more for laboratory-based research rather than for the desk-based or fieldwork variety.
Equipment	The majority of sponsors will cover costs that have been specifically identified as essential for execution and completion of the research project.

FINANCIAL CONSIDERATIONS FOR ALL RESEARCHERS

Consideration of Table 2 should by now have convinced you that all researchers, no matter how novice, have to be conversant with the financial aspects of conducting research, while even experienced researchers seeking *research funding* would do well to obtain the advice of experts who are often found in Research Support centres within universities. All funders are seeking value for money so they will only fund those project proposals which demonstrate that the project is addressing a problem that can realistically be solved, and which has a carefully prepared budget that covers all essentials in a prudent way. Such prudence takes into account the sustainability of research and other activities in Higher Education, so that efforts are made to ensure that the full cost of the project is covered, with no detriment to other research projects and teaching activities.

Similarly, reviewers for funding organisations will be alert to the real costs of research so will not countenance any attempt to 'pad out' costs. On the contrary, they will expect all costs to be fully justified so you need to be clear about how much must be spent and why. This is the essence of research accountability. This accountability goes two ways – it is as much a fault to underestimate costs as to overestimate them, by mistake or intent in each case. Whether you simply forget an item of expenditure, or get its value wrong, or cut costs in order to provide a more competitive bid, you risk raising concerns in the reviewers that you are too inexperienced, or foolhardy, or that you will run into trouble with your funded project when money becomes tight. On the other hand, reviewers will be equally sceptical of exaggerated costs or attempts made, by those expecting funders to trim budgets, to provide something innocuous/superfluous for them to cut in the mistaken expectation that 'they are bound to want to cut something'. A tightly calculated and argued budget is much more likely to succeed, or at least to add to your reputation as a researcher, than a tactical or sloppy one.

Those of you who are preparing a proposal for a *research degree* place may at this point like to proceed to the next chapter or simply skim-read the following sections as guidance for the future, for the rest of this chapter concentrates on the important detail required by those preparing a proposal for *research funding.*

ACTIVITY 17 PRODUCING A ROUGH ESTIMATE OF RESEARCH COSTS

Before we work on how to achieve such tight budgeting, review your emerging project plan now and try to produce a rough estimate of costs, identifying the items/resources required, how much you think you will need of each and then how much each will cost. You can then review this estimate later in comparison to further estimates produced at the end of the chapter so that you can either feel proud of your financial prowess or be alert to items you might forget or miscalculate.

TYPES AND STYLES OF BUDGETS FOR FUNDING APPLICATIONS

Each funder has different conditions and requirements regarding layout and inclusions/exclusions for financial information, and these may change over time, especially in the climate of austerity prevailing at the time of writing. Therefore it is important that you use the information in this book as a guide but also check the details of current requirements for the range of funders to whom you are considering applying. It is likely that some funders will provide a form, or fixed format, and they will use terms that you should familiarise yourself with. Although we will include some of these in the Glossary at the back of the book, for ease of reference while reading this chapter the main terms related to research budgets are included in Box 14, most of which have been compiled from those found on several Research Council websites as listed in Appendix 1 and accessed in May 2011, or are based on such information.

BOX 14 COMMON DEFINITIONS RELATED TO BUDGETS

- **Grant**: This is the common term for the financial support of a project which tends to cover only a proportion of its full economic cost. A **research grant** is the term used to denote the financial contribution made towards a research project by a funding organisation using its own assessment procedures and criteria.
- **Grant holder**: This is the individual who is allocated the grant and who has intellectual and managerial responsibility for it. The common name for this person is Principal Investigator or PI.
- **Co-investigator**: This person has some level of joint responsibility, with the PI, for the project in terms of its management and intellectual leadership.
- **Research organisation**: This is the organisation which employs the PI and which is responsible for the administration of the awarded grant. It is this accountability, in addition to other help based on experience, that makes it critically important to engage the institution's research accounting team in the proposal development and bidding process.
- **Full economic cost (fEC)**: This is the total cost, which includes direct and indirect costs and an overhead cost, as well as a contribution to a recurring investment in the research institution's infrastructure.
- **Directly incurred costs**: These are identifiable costs, evidenced by an audit record of invoices and receipts, that can be traced as specifically arising from the conduct of the research and are debited from the grant as the actual cash value spent.
- **Directly allocated costs**: Some resources used by a project may be shared with other projects or research activities, for instance, the running costs of equipment or the costs of bulk orders. An estimate of the proportion of the cost applicable to the funded project is made and this is charged as an allocated rather than directly incurred cost.
- **Indirect costs**: This is a calculated proportion of a range of costs that are charged to all projects that have not otherwise been included in the directly allocated costs, and which may include the costs of departmental or institution-wide administration and services such as library and IT departments.
- **Transparent Approach to Costing (TRAC)**: This is a methodology agreed and used by universities and research bodies in HE to calculate full economic costs.

Please note that, while it is important for researchers to know the full cost of their research, few funders will provide all elements of a **full economic costing** so it is important to read very carefully their guidelines for completing your budget. In these they will also tell you whether they require itemised budgets, with a line for each item of costs usually separated under headings of personnel and operational costs, or a functional budget that aggregates expenditure under each research objective. Below we will summarise the kinds of things that should be included under the headings of personnel and operating costs, but note that the cost of consultants such as specialist information technology experts might be included under either heading, so again check the guidance notes of your preferred funding body. However, it is important, wherever they are included, that their inclusion should particularly enhance the proposal rather than seeming to substitute for key deficits in the main research team. You might, for instance, make judicious and limited use of very specific expertise that would provide an additional perspective or skill.

KEY ELEMENTS OF THE BUDGET: PERSONNEL

Personnel costs usually constitute the largest part of a project budget (unless you are bidding for high-energy physics projects which require large, expensive equipment) so we will deal with them first. These costs are a proportion of the salaries and 'on costs' (National Insurance and/or pension contributions and/or other costs covered by the employer) of the people contributing to the project. First, identify who is really needed to ensure the project is completed successfully and then calculate the percentage involvement or effort required of each. This part must be comprehensively justified so try to produce named people whose CVs demonstrate that their contribution both is essential and strengthens the bid. A team member noted as 'not yet identified/appointed' and therefore to be advised (TBA) later will make your proposal vulnerable to trimming. The following role descriptions may help you decide whom you might need and for what purpose.

Project Director/Principal Investigator (PI): Usually this is the author of the proposal who will have responsibility for the administration and intellectual rigour of the research project. This grand title may apply to you if this is not a proposal that you are drafting, as a post-doctoral researcher or similar, for your mentor or research leader. Whoever takes this role, it is important to ensure that the percentage effort of this lead person indicates a high quality of effort and commitment and includes time spent engaged in the research itself and also in supervising others, managing the process and disseminating the results. Usually this person is not employed full time on the project, having teaching and/or management and other duties for the organisation, so this becomes a directly allocated cost rather than a directly incurred cost. Thus the time spent on the project is calculated at an hourly rate, often one that is agreed by the organisation/institution and involves a justified percentage of the **full-time equivalent** (FTE) salary for that specified point on the salary scale.

Co-investigator: This is usually someone who shares the intellectual responsibility for the project and may have some specific administrative responsibilities that should be noted and accounted for in their time allocation in the same way as for the PI. Their costs would also be calculated in the same way as for the PI.

Research Assistant/Post-doctoral Fellow/Research Associate: Members of staff with titles such as these are those involved in the main data collection and they may have involvement in both the initial drafting of the proposal and the dissemination of results. If they are employed full time on the project, or at least for a contracted amount of time, then they are counted under directly incurred costs, whereas if they have other responsibilities beyond the project in their work then a calculation of directly allocated cost must be made and defended.

Professional staff for particular activities, for example, *a statistician*: this may be a consultant (see note above) and so may be a directly incurred cost, or someone who provides a central or departmental service, in which case there is likely to be an agreed institutional project rate for this service.

Technicians: unless this is a very specialist project that requires the employment for a fixed and specified time of a technician, it is likely that the technician time will be service time, a directly allocated cost.

Secretary/Administrator: Again, unless this project involves a heavy and specified clerical component for which an appointment for the project period is made, the normal clerical and administrative duties for a project such as booking appointments, organising travel and venues for meetings, etc. should be met by a directly allocated cost which should be strongly justified if it is not to be particularly vulnerable to trimming.

For all these posts it is important to ensure that you select someone with the appropriate expertise for the job rather than someone 'cheap' (but not having the requisite skills, including necessary gravitas) in order to gain the grant/funding. Equally, do not select someone expensive in the hope that this will provide extra financial leeway or gravitas for your project. It can be tempting to include a 'famous name' in order to impress the reviewers but this will not help if it makes the results of the project needlessly expensive to achieve.

Do remember to include any increments that may be accrued to salaries over the duration of the project (though any other pay rises will not generally be funded). For your project to be credible you should detail specific contributions and responsibilities within a tight but realistic costing framework so that the funder is able to judge exactly what they are paying for and can confidently expect as an outcome. They will be looking for value for money but equally will be reluctant to invest in a project that is likely to founder through poor budget predictions. Similar caveats apply to costing operating costs.

KEY ELEMENTS OF THE BUDGET: OPERATING COSTS

These include all communication costs within the project such as printing, mailing, phone, video conferencing facilities, and related office supplies. If some office equipment is required for the specific and sole use by the project there may be an allowance made for rent, hire or purchase of it, but, as for computers and similar equipment, usually only depreciation costs apply.

Similarly, funders will expect that some other equipment will already exist in the institution – although they will expect that you use the correct equipment for the task, they are highly unlikely to pay for the establishment of a new laboratory or interview suite so budgeting for equipment needs some careful consideration. For instance, they are likely to look more favourably on a sensitive budget that proposes the hiring or sharing of specialist equipment. You will, however, be expected to claim for instruments that deteriorate with use or require re-honing or calibrating, for example, or for equipment that will be for the exclusive use of the project. For very expensive equipment you may need to provide several quotations from a range of sources or, indeed, this special equipment may be counted under the heading 'exceptional items', though this requires an exceptionally good case for inclusion.

For consumables, you should also carefully estimate the quantity required, and present the rationale for it. This section should include stationery as well as specialist materials such as chemicals, glassware, biological supplies, animals and sufficient animal feed. You should show your working-out to the extent of multiplying the number/amount required of each of these by the specific unit cost so that you can present a sound and precisely justified figure that is less likely to be trimmed than a vague one.

If your project involves essential travel and a contribution towards subsistence then you should clearly identify specified modes of travel, with justification, and observe the limits supplied either in your institutional guidance or by the funder for specific travel, accommodation and meal costs. A wise budget will indicate that travel will serve several purposes or be arranged so that several locations at one time are fitted into one journey (collecting information from adjacent or consecutive geographical sources, for instance) and/or might combine several important features or activities for the project, for example, a preliminary dissemination opportunity combined with further data collection. Some projects may incur other expenses, such as the reimbursement of travel costs or other expenses to volunteers; the provision of incentives to participate; maintenance costs of equipment; software licences; or fees to access archives. It is wise to consider how essential these are to the successful completion of the project and have that rationale ready when you contact the funders to check if these are indeed allowable, if they have not specifically mentioned them in their guidance notes.

A number of these items might be provided by your department (e.g. the maintenance or licence costs) so, rather than try to recoup that expense, you could note it as an 'in kind' cost or a contribution from your institution. Some funders do require some matching contribution either 'in kind' or actual financial support so keep in mind things such as volunteers' time or goods and services provided to the project by other sponsors when considering the limits to and justification of your budget.

It may be necessary to find more than one funder for your project. You must make explicit the elements each is funding of the budget (no double counting or charging), not just allocate a proportion of the total to each. There are, though, some items that few funders will support – these are listed in Box 15.

BOX 15 EXPENSES THAT ARE SELDOM RECOGNISED BY FUNDERS

- Full costs of established academic staff – it is expected that only a proportion of their time will contribute to the project.
- Hospitality or entertainment unless it is an incentive to participants (e.g. coffee and buns while taking part in a focus group).
- Travel for general study purposes rather than for fieldwork or an agreed dissemination activity.
- Books that can be readily obtained from a library.
- Contingency or miscellaneous expenditure.

Note that UK Research Councils only pay about 80 percent of fEC. Charitable foundations tend not to pay direct or indirect costs, and the EU has its own rules that vary over time. Check the current position with your local research and enterprise or research accounting office.

THE BUDGET AFTER SUBMISSION OF THE PROPOSAL

Budgetary concerns do not end with the submission of your proposal; they will form a pervasive aspect of your research project from inception to completion. For instance, let us assume now that you receive the good news that your project proposal has been approved. That is not the end of your financial concerns. For instance, it may be approved but the grant given may be less than the amount you requested. If you did, as advised, budget very carefully then you must resist the immediate celebratory response while you re-consider, even more carefully, whether you can actually achieve the agreed aims and objectives within the bounds of a more stringent budget without compromising the quality of the work and the product. Remember that your reputation rests on this. Be prepared to negotiate, in a respectful but firm way, to perhaps reduce the scope of the project in a sensible manner to meet the financial restrictions. It is all too easy early in your career to fall into the trap of selling your expertise cheaply in order to get a foot on the ladder, so seek advice from more experienced colleagues before selling your soul to the lowest bidder!

You would be wise, too, to check the guidance notes or with the funder directly about how flexible you can be with any allocated funding in terms of whether virement is allowed. Virement is the transfer of one budget line to another – something that really should only be used with a legitimate rationale such as the early purchase of goods to get a better price or the change of a procedure to a more effective one that only becomes apparent at a later stage of the work. Do avoid asking the question if it is likely to sound as if your budgeting was inaccurate in the first place. Moreover, you should be aware that significant changes to a project once funding has been agreed will require consideration of the potential effects on other aspects of the procedure so formal approval must be sought. In the next chapter on project management we will discuss planning a degree of flexibility to cope with unforeseen challenges to your carefully honed research plan.

Remember that a good budget is one which is carefully calculated, with attention paid to both propriety and quality of outcome, but also one that is realistic.

ACTIVITY 18 PRODUCING A MORE DETAILED BUDGET

We hope that the information provided above will help you to compile a realistic budget. This would be a good time to consider producing a draft of that budget to compare with your previous estimate (Activity 13), both to determine if there are items you neglected to count or over-estimated in value and to help you determine which source or sources of funding are likely to be responsive to the cost as well as the topic and aim of your proposed research. Bear in mind that funders have restricted funding ranges at different times.

This is also a good time to introduce yourself and your project ideas to the staff in the institutional research accounting office, who will guide you further and provide expert, up-to-date advice about both institutional and funding body requirements.

REFLECTION POINT: DOES YOUR PROPOSED RESEARCH OUTCOME JUSTIFY ITS COST?

Now is a crunch point (yet another) when you should consider whether the results and outcome of your proposed research will justify its cost. It may be that the fEC figure seems too high even if the results would be interesting. On the other hand, it may be that the results would be very substantial but the cost is more than you can obtain full funding for. However, all is not lost if either is the case because you could at this point consider how you could adjust the number of your objectives and/or your methodology and/or the scale of your project so that your financial requirements become more realistic. It is better to do this now than submit your proposal regardless and risk wasting the germ of a good idea.

8

WHAT PLANNING AND ORGANISATION DETAILS ARE REQUIRED?

CHAPTER OVERVIEW

This chapter discusses:

- the planning of goals and establishment of deadlines;
- managing time on a project effectively;
- implementing plans;
- research governance;
- people management;
- schedules and timelines.

ESTABLISHING GOALS AND DEADLINES

In Chapter 3 we noted the need to organise and plan in advance the complex activity of preparing a proposal. In this chapter we will use the same principles as we urge you to consider how you should demonstrate your organisational ability through a project plan. As with most of the previous chapters we will begin this one by addressing first those of you who are at the stage of applying for a university place on a *doctoral degree*. By this time you will recognise that, like those who are seeking funding for a proposed research project which is not part of a higher degree, this section of a proposal contains aspects crucial to convincing reviewers of the credibility of your plans and also serves to ensure that you embark on a practically feasible undertaking. At the end of the previous chapter we urged you to consider whether the financial cost of the project was justified by the achievement of its aims and objectives. Now we are asking you to evaluate whether the investment of time and energy can be sensibly organised so that the aims and objectives can be achieved within a reasonable – or, indeed, required – timescale.

It is tempting, of course, whatever form your envisioned project takes, *doctoral degree* or *funded research*, to set an ambitious set of goals in an attempt to impress your reviewers, but in this section of your proposal you must demonstrate that these goals are achievable. To do this you need to provide a clear plan of what you intend to do, how long each step will take, how you will know when you have successfully negotiated each step, and how the steps fit together to meet the final objective. For doctoral study, in some respects such a plan is easier to begin because some aspects are predetermined by institutional requirements. In general in the UK, and increasingly so across Europe, institutions set limits on registration time that match with a criterion for assessment: that the product of the doctorate should be that which can be achieved within the equivalent of three years of full-time independent study. On the other hand, most UK research councils fund doctoral study for four years (full time), in recognition that writing up and attendance to generic skills training will require time in addition to project completion.

In the Appendices you will find information about research council websites and publications that describe the course of the doctorate to help you plan for specific milestones in your study such as annual reviews, and also the process that is variously called transfer/upgrade/confirmation that takes place about a third of the way through the process in order to evaluate whether the research is likely to produce an 'original contribution to knowledge', another main assessment criterion for the doctorate. Although you are unlikely to be managing other people during a doctoral project, except for your relationship with your supervisor (see next chapter), the more general discussion about planning and managing your research that follows will be relevant to you and will help you ground your research in practicality.

Those of you working towards a *funded research project* without the constraints and check points involved in a research degree will need to establish your own deadlines within a balanced programme that considers economy (time is money) and practical feasibility. Some clues about how to achieve this now follow with recognition that this is a personal as well as a professional challenge.

PROJECT PLANNING AND TIME MANAGEMENT

All research or project management is based on a transparent, coherent plan of action that delineates for the achievement of objectives:

- what needs to be done, what tasks and activities are involved with explicit targets for achievement;
- when these should start and be completed, in what order;
- who is responsible for their achievement.

This plan should reflect careful and informed decision-making if it is to serve to justify all the resources requested (personnel, equipment and other expenses) in the budget and to convince reviewers of the proposer's capacity to complete the project effectively and successfully. While there is no set formula for good and effective management, and we recognise that there are many different leadership styles and methods of working, there are certain pieces of information and ways of setting it out that will help with this task of convincing others. We will present these below and also alert you to critical procedural activities that you should consider. First, we urge you to reflect on your normal 'modus operandi': how you usually work and what keeps you going. This will help you to orientate your formal plan towards one which will be comfortable for you to operate.

ACTIVITY 19 IDENTIFYING YOUR PREVIOUSLY SUCCESSFUL PLANNING APPROACHES

Think back through projects (of any kind, not necessarily research projects) with which you have been engaged, and focus on one or two in which you have been in the lead in some way and have had some success. (Later, you might want to consider some less successful ones to identify what actions/attitudes/approaches to avoid but for now concentrate on relatively successful ones.) Try to identify what approach you took that made the project successful. For instance, was the project tightly organised, well structured and methodical in operation or were you working under pressure, juggling several key things at once? While none of us perform well if very stressed, there is no doubt that some of us (we comment from experience!) perform at our best when adrenalin is flowing from facing challenges.

Realistically, there are few worthwhile research projects that flow from start to finish smoothly and without challenge. Yet you must remain in control of the project rather than the project controlling your life. So consider as you read on how you can organise your project to remain stimulating yet be ordered enough to fit your personal preferred approach and natural work pattern – and then consider how much flexibility needs to be built in to cope with the vicissitudes of life such as unexpected illness or changing work responsibilities.

Before we leave the personal aspects to get down to practicalities related to the research project, do remember that your research activities have to fit in a life full of other demands and obligations, some of which are unpredictable, so be careful to calculate your commitment to fit into your normal work time only – then at least you will have some leeway to fit in some 'overtime' if plans go a little awry.

IMPLEMENTATION PLANS

Planning, as you might guess, can be helped by first making lists. One of these should be of your strategic goals – what sub-goals must be achieved on the path to achieving your aims and objectives (refer back to chapter 5). Reviewing your research design (see Chapter 6) will help with providing the detail of this. Another list might be of the people involved in your research other than yourself (see the next chapter) and their likely availability, while you also might need to collate a list of required regular meetings or documentation points. These last are a facet of all researchers' lives; students must produce annual reports of progress and summary documents for transfer/upgrade/confirmation processes, while other researchers are often required to make regular progress reports. These are usually linked to targets, such as achieving a certain amount of data, or may be used to mark the completion dates for key milestones, or be required for meetings of Review or Steering Groups (for more on this, refer to the next chapter). Perhaps we should also add a list of potential hazards that might affect your research so that you can be alert for their occurrence, anticipate any resultant changes to your plan, and build in sufficient flexibility to reduce their impact or allow for negotiation of a revised plan.

All of these things need to be woven together into the coherent plan of action that will guide your research and indicate its feasibility to others. Box 16 provides the names of most of the important aspects that may need to be incorporated into that plan, depending on your discipline area; it will be up to you to decide where they fit, and for how long, in your schedule of work, though we will follow on with some suggestions.

BOX 16 ELEMENTS OF A PROJECT PLAN

- Gaining ethical approval and/or permissions for access
- Recruiting, selecting and training staff
- Checking health and safety aspects
- Booking time for use of instruments or equipment or access to documents
- Organising and booking expert support
- Conducting an ongoing literature review
- Laboratory or fieldwork or deskwork

- Maintaining records
- Routine project/team meetings
- Writing interim reports
- Organising and attending external review meetings, including travel
- Analysing data
- Interpreting the results
- Evaluating the research
- Writing the final report
- Disseminating the findings.

This list indicates that there are issues of both research governance and people management that may need to be taken into account.

RESEARCH GOVERNANCE

This term refers to all the aspects of research related to the process of ensuring good practice in research as required by institutions' and funding bodies' codes of good research practice. It includes: gaining necessary permissions; adhering to the highest standards of integrity (see the discussion on ethics in Chapter 6); and making certain that your work conforms to legal obligations. This involves declarations of conflicts of interest, ensuring the health and safety of your fellow workers and all others involved in the research process, and also meeting the requirements of the Data Protection Act. The eight principles of that Act are summarised in Box 17.

BOX 17 THE EIGHT PRINCIPLES OF THE DATA PROTECTION ACT 1998

Personal data must be:

- Processed fairly and lawfully.
- Processed only for one or more specified and lawful purposes.
- Adequate, relevant and not excessive for those purposes.
- Accurate and kept up to date – subjects have the right to have inaccurate personal data corrected or destroyed if the personal information is inaccurate to any matter of fact.
- Kept for no longer than is necessary for the purposes it is being processed.
- Processed in line with the rights of individuals – this includes the right to be informed of all the information held about them, to prevent processing of their personal information

(Continued)

(Continued)

for marketing purposes, and to compensation if they can prove they have been damaged by a data controller's non-compliance with the Act.

- Secured against accidental loss, destruction or damage and against unauthorised or unlawful processing – this applies to you even if your organisation uses a third party to process personal information on your behalf.
- Not transferred to countries outside the European Economic Area – the EU plus Norway, Iceland and Liechtenstein – that do not have adequate protection for individuals' personal information, unless a condition from Schedule 4 of the Act can be met.

Ethics procedures can be very lengthy, as we indicated earlier, so it is important that this process is attended to as soon as funding is agreed. Some funders may expect that some effort to gain ethical approval in principle has already been made.

PEOPLE MANAGEMENT

Being a Principal Investigator in a project that involves the contribution of other researchers implies that leadership skills are needed to ensure that procedures are adhered to, deadlines are met, records are kept, standards maintained and, last but not least, motivation is preserved. Although you may be excited about your project (indeed you should be at this stage), the vast majority of research does include some aspects that can be tedious, and it is not unusual for researchers to have occasional periods when their morale needs boosting for one reason or another. It is the leader's role to spot these occasions and provide that needed lift of spirits.

As you may recall from the budget outlines in the previous chapter, part of the research plan is a clear account of key staff, their roles, functions and responsibilities and the reporting structure. These should be documented so that everyone knows what they are responsible for and how their work interrelates with that of others. If you are the Principal Investigator you will have the major responsibility for intellectual leadership, and will be accountable for the budget. In all countries there is likely to be an expectation that the lead researcher encourages and supports the development of other members of their research team but in the UK all the major research funders have subscribed to the principles of a concordat to support the career development of researchers. Research institutions provide, usually through their human resources departments, opportunities for personal and professional development – see Box 1. You will be expected by many funders to describe in your final report the training that has been engaged in by your team so it does form an important part of your action plan. Such training provision and other support for the development of your team should also be incorporated into your plan for the production of your proposal, for it may well have budgetary implications (training may or may not be locally available and/or free).

BOX 18 THE CONCORDAT TO SUPPORT THE CAREER DEVELOPMENT OF RESEARCHERS 2008: KEY PRINCIPLES

1 Recognition of the importance of recruiting, selecting and retaining researchers with the highest potential to achieve excellence in research.
2 Researchers are recognised and valued by their employing organisation as an essential part of their organisation's human resources and a key component of their overall strategy to develop and deliver world-class research.
3 Researchers are equipped and supported to be adaptable and flexible in an increasingly diverse, mobile, global research environment.
4 The importance of researchers' personal and career development, and lifelong learning, is clearly recognised and promoted at all stages of their career.
5 Individual researchers share the responsibility for and need to pro-actively engage in their own personal and career development, and lifelong learning.
6 Diversity and equality must be promoted in all aspects of the recruitment and career management of researchers.
7 The sector and all stakeholders will undertake regular and collective review of their progress in strengthening the attractiveness and sustainability of research careers in the UK.

SCHEDULES AND TIMELINES

Earlier we noted all the tasks that you might need to include in your action plan, and it was probably obvious to you that these, while falling into some kind of logical order, do not follow each other sequentially. Some activities, like the literature review and the maintaining of records, span the whole time allocated to the project while others recur intermittently, such as routine team meetings and meetings with review or steering committees. Yet others are dependent on the results of earlier activities (such as the study of artefacts following the gaining of approved access to them, interviews with participants following the gaining of permissions from appropriate authorities and the signing of a confidentiality agreement, the conduct of one experiment being dependent on the results of a prior one) and will occur over time. Although this kind of information can be conveyed in the form of a table with an 'activity' heading in one column and 'duration' and 'dates' heading others, it is often helpful to readers, and indeed to you and your team while planning and implementing the research, to have a visual display in the form of a spreadsheet or timeline. In Chapter 3 we suggested that you might use a flow chart that demonstrates which activities must precede others, which occur simultaneously and which result from earlier ones. Some funders specifically ask you to identify 'milestones' in the process when certain stages of the project will be completed. These may be used for timing formal reporting and review meetings, the latter usually involving an external, expert reviewer. These can be very helpful in giving you a sense of achievement but also for providing you with advice in the light of unexpected developments in your project.

Another common form of illustrating the progress of your research is a Gantt chart, a simple example of which you can see in Figure 1. Your first draft of such a chart with only key aspects of the fieldwork/lab work included will give you an indication of when milestones might occur, when you might need to organise for such things as expert advice or hire of equipment and, an important element in a lengthy project, vacation times for you and your staff.

Another benefit of a visual plot such as this is that you can more readily see where it is important to incorporate:

- time for reflection, where creative work is required;
- times for particular activities that are dependent on availability of participants (for example, the academic terms or semesters for teachers) or natural cycles (for example, growth periods in agriculture);
- anticipation of extra support needs during times of pressure;
- plans to distribute duties across the team when there are activities occurring simultaneously.

Now is the time to test your research design for practical viability in the time you have available.

ACTIVITY 20 PREPARING A GANTT CHART

Using your list of research activities and referring to Box 16 for guidance, prepare a Gantt chart spread over the time you judge you will require. Try different versions to avoid pressure points as far as possible and try not to forget the impact that holidays, celebration times and cyclical events can have on researchers, participants and availability of important research materials and equipment. Include in it some indication of important milestones in your project.

Mapping exercise	x	X	X	x																			
Survey instrument preparation		x	X	x	x																		
Survey administered						x	x	x															
Map prepared		x	X	x	x	x																	
Analysis of survey, identification of cases							x	x		x	x	x	x										
Analysis of cases													x	x	x	x	x	x	x	x			
Derivation of models																			x		x	X	
Reports written							x						x			x				x		x	x
Dissemination events								x		x					x		x				x		X
Months	O	N	D	J	F	M	A	M	J	J	A	S	O	N	D	J	F	M	A	M	J	J	A

FIGURE 1 Gantt chart showing activities plotted over 23 months, October to August

The final point to be made in this chapter, and one for you to reflect on, is that funders are particularly keen on timely completion of projects and may have firm plans in place for dissemination or for announcements. While it is therefore extremely important that you plan the process carefully, its phases and the deadlines involved, and then do the utmost to maintain the schedule, it is also important to recognise slippage and deal with it in good time; hence the value of a visible chart throughout the life of the project. If that slippage is irremediable, then the funders would value prompt negotiation of a revised final deadline rather than being faced by a late submission.

Your future reputation as a researcher will also benefit if you can give good cause in unusual circumstances for any delay in completion and show responsibility by providing an alternative plan that can be implemented. However, it is better yet never to find yourself in that position so give careful consideration to building in an appropriate degree of flexibility. Taking the advice of more experienced colleagues in your field can be helpful with this, as with other aspects of producing a research proposal. We turn to the value of collaboration in the next chapter.

REFLECTION POINT: INJECTING A NOTE OF REALISM

The aim of all this careful planning should be an efficiently run project, but efficiency can only be achieved if you have given some consideration to yourself and your significant others. Make sure that your plan is realistic and includes some time for refreshment and reflection!

9

WHO ARE THE OTHER POTENTIAL CONTRIBUTORS TO AND REFEREES FOR YOUR PROJECT?

CHAPTER OVERVIEW

This chapter discusses:

- building professional relationships;
- making contacts and seeking help;
- developing partnerships and collaborations;
- the review process and what reviewers are seeking;
- preparing for their response.

BUILDING PROFESSIONAL RELATIONSHIPS

Although research is often a lonely activity, especially for those embarking on a research degree that requires the demonstration of considerable autonomy, no researcher should underestimate the value of seeking the help of others at key points. In the longer term it is the opinions of others, experts in research, that will determine whether or not you gain a degree place or funding for your project. So although your academic experience might lead you first to turn to books, in this book we urge you also to make good use of that other important resource – people. Which people are best approached at which time is the subject of our next section, which will follow the course of preparing your project for submission. Later we will address what will happen to your proposal once submitted, considering the people who will review it and what they will be looking for.

In this chapter there is little to differentiate those seeking a degree place and those seeking funding for research. There are nuanced differences which we will note as we go along but the message is generally similar – make, maintain and respond positively to personal contacts. Whether you are planning to embark on a degree programme or are seeking funding, you will serve your cause best by building professional relationships in your field; this process is an iterative, reciprocal one that takes time and consideration of others. Of course, this means that better, more helpful professional relationships will be there to help you in the future but you must begin the process as soon as you become interested in pursuing research. In the following sections we provide some clues about how to get started.

BUILDING ON OVERVIEWS OF REQUIREMENTS

In Chapters 2 and 3 we introduced the notion that different institutions and organisations have their own preferences for the content and structure of applications that involve research proposals, and urged you to become familiar with the criteria of several organisations with research interests in your field. You might at this point find it helpful to refer back to the results you produced for Activities 1, 4 and 5 in which you began your identification of potential contacts and their attributes/requirements. We hope that this chapter will enable you to build on that personal resource. As a reminder, we noted for potential research students that both institutions and departments within them will have regulations and guidelines for proposals, some with very specific requirements, perhaps about content areas, while others may be more general, such as 'demonstrating a previous engagement with the topic'. Once you are familiar with these and have some ideas in mind for research then it is time to contact potential supervisors, but consider the points in the next section first.

Similarly, bodies that fund research (research councils, foundations, charities and so on) provide funding guides that delineate the sort of research they are interested in and the nature of proposals they are seeking. It is worthwhile exploring their websites in detail, noting important clues to both explicit and implicit selection criteria embedded in their mission statements, strategic plans and current themes, and recently funded research, perhaps even in transcripts of talks that their officers have given at conferences, such as those run by the UK Council for Graduate Education (UKCGE: www.ukcge.ac.uk), the Society for Research in Higher Education (SRHE: www.srhe.ac.uk) and Vitae (www.vitae.ac.uk), as well as conferences in your own discipline. As you gain more experience you could enhance your understanding of their objectives and preferences to your longer-term benefit if you were to volunteer in the future as a reviewer of proposals yourself so that you can monitor how their interests develop.

Having collected salient information from the documents provided by institutions/funders, including important dates for submission, formats required, length restrictions and other such unambiguous quantitative data, you must then seek clarification about how your ideas might fit with their remit. From the website you should be able to identify a contact number of someone involved in your general discipline area. You will find that these people are open to enquiries from prospective applicants, and very willing to provide advice, elaborate on requirements and give guidance on procedures. Such people are unlikely to be reviewers of submissions at the discipline level but they will be keen to avoid people, the proposers and reviewers, wasting time preparing or reading proposals that do not have the required information in the preferred format. Before phoning, be prepared to ask focussed questions by making contact first with helpers closer to home.

MAKING CONTACTS AND SEEKING HELP

As you begin to formulate your ideas, give them more substance by discussing them with colleagues and friends and then write them down to give to peers and mentors to comment on. Requesting feedback on these tentative ruminations can make you feel very vulnerable but this is an essential component of all research, one that will become familiar, but no less painful, as your career develops. It helps to refine your thoughts and develop more fruitful pathways as misunderstandings, mistakes and impractical notions are identified and discarded. One of the main benefits of belonging to a research group, formal or informal, is that it can be a safe forum for flying the kites of ideas that may turn out to be either ridiculous or inspired.

As your ideas become more refined, seek out a wider range of feedback, particularly from more experienced, successful researchers both within your field and outside it. The former will be able to alert you to recent and relevant research in the area while the latter act as intelligent others, similar to the eventual review panel, who can provide an evaluation of how clearly you have explained your ideas, how well you have argued your case, and how convincing and engaging your proposal is.

If you are seeking financial support then this is the time, too, to make contact with your research support office, which can help with practicalities such as alerting you to the time-consuming nature of the preparation of some electronic formats for submission as well as the period they need for dealing with internal budgeting issues. You should also, at this point, be negotiating with your head of department regarding their willingness to support your application and any subsequent research activity. Your plans need to fit in with the general departmental or school plans. It is in everyone's best interests that these plans articulate well, so this discussion will centre on your own availability for other duties and the availability of resources for your use in the project proposed.

You might also explore any possibilities of financial support or sponsorship with private sector organisations – business and industry. Formal applications usually follow from informal discussion with a key contact, an insider who will be your advocate. Such contacts can be found in a variety of ways: reading the relevant journals, attending conferences, talking to the organisation's recruiters at job fairs; talking to employees who are members of institutional advisory board, to alumni now working with the company, or to colleagues who have established links already. These relationships require some nurturing; it is not simply a case of identifying a key person and submitting a proposal. Their available funding and interest may fluctuate with the national economy but building a strong relationship can be a source not just of funding for research or studentships but of research contexts, participants or equipment.

When working with other organisations, in the private or public sector, it is important to establish a reciprocal relationship so that you contribute as well as seek support. Try to go beyond contractual obligations to share results, useful information from the literature, expertise and friendly banter with gatekeepers in the organisation, if that is your style, so that you can build a relationship of mutual professional support for the future.

DEVELOPING COLLABORATIONS AND PARTNERSHIPS

Collaborations and partnerships in research can be long-standing or exist only for one particular project. Whichever is the case, credibility can be boosted for all parties if each contributes something unique to the exercise and there is added value in working together. Even those new to research can bring expertise, perhaps methodological, or a new theoretical perspective or simply enthusiasm and motivation, while a more experienced colleague can add weight by reputation and experience. It may be that you need to seek out particular expertise for a specific aspect of the project but take care to establish, through preliminary informal discussion, an understanding of the needs and expected contributions of each partner.

Developing trust at this stage, which allows for frank sharing of ideas and concerns when the project is underway, is a fundamental prerequisite for a successful outcome of the project in a timely fashion. Many long-standing, successful and famous research partnerships have started in this way then led to project series and publications with partners alternating as lead researchers as they stimulate each other's ideas and provide stability in a fairly turbulent profession.

Then again, it is not only for establishing working partnerships that it is important to get to know others and their work in your professional and discipline area. All project proposers will be expected to nominate one or more referees to attest to their experience, expertise and potential in relation to the project. It is important, therefore, that you keep in touch with people who are or have been familiar with both your academic work and your attributes (such as your ability to work with others, focus on the task, fulfil obligations and so forth). Such people, especially previous mentors, significant teachers and employers, will need up-to-date information in order to provide a supportive reference so it is sensible to maintain contact by sending papers you have published or information about your new job, etc. This is part of the professional skill of networking, a skill particularly important for researchers because it can be mutually supportive as you keep each other up to date with recent research and publications. Part of that skill is simple good manners. While people might tolerate being asked by you to provide a reference although they have not heard from you for some time previously, they are likely to be less positive about responding to a request out of the blue from an institution or funding organisation. Nominated referees are significant aspects of your proposal so do not neglect them and do inform them of the details of your proposal. Bear in mind that creating a sound, relevant and tactical reference is a time-consuming and skilled task, while it is relatively easy to respond with an unconsidered and out-of-date one.

Similarly, you need to be tactical if you intend to respond to a funder's call for proposals related to a particular topic; you need to consider who are the likely other responders, your potential competitors. If you are familiar with their work and style then you have an increased chance of devising ways of making your own proposal significantly different for it to stand out in a crowd in a positive way. Alternatively, you might consider contacting one or more of these potential competitors with a view to presenting a collaborative bid, strengthened by the expertise you both contribute, and impressing reviewers with your shared commitment.

ACTIVITY 21 BUILDING A RESOURCE LIST OF CONTACTS

This is a good point to consolidate your list of professional contacts, consider the roles they might play in your proposed research and consider how you might develop your relationships further. You might like to brainstorm the names of all the people in your research and professional area with whom you have had contact recently, say in the last year, then trawl your memory or email contact list, conference attendance lists, facebook contacts or similar for those you met at conferences or worked with in the past. You could then sort these under headings such as potential 'research collaborators', 'advisors', 'referees' and 'competitors', remembering that some names might appear on more than one list. Significantly, some might be called upon by the funding organisation as peer reviewers of your proposal so it will be advantageous to build your reputation further by updating them on your developing expertise and research passions.

We will now turn specifically to the reviewing process and then consider the role and functions of those important people, project reviewers, and how you can interact productively with them.

THE REVIEW PROCESS

If your proposal is for a university place for a *research degree* then the process is likely to follow a fairly standard procedure in which an administrator, usually a senior-faculty-level person, checks practical and factual details such as whether your academic qualifications and any professional or language achievements meet the requirements for admission, and whether the topic fits within any of the discipline areas in the institution. The documents including your proposal will then go to a senior academic in the relevant subject area/s for a decision about whether there is a team of suitable supervisors available. It will be these academics, perhaps with their senior colleague, who will review your proposal.

If you are also hoping to submit your proposal for *funding* through either an internal (university or departmental) or external studentship process, the reviewers as prospective supervisors may help you, if they are impressed by your credentials and interested in your topic area, to refine the proposal further to enhance its chances of success. For external studentships they will be required to provide details of their own research record and particularly to make a case that they provide excellent facilities and support/guidance for their research students. (In some cases, in the sciences in particular, they are likely to have identified a research topic in advance so the balance of input into the project design will be more towards your tailoring their choice of topic and general approach towards your own specific interests and expertise. This is in contrast to your generating an original research idea yourself as may frequently, but not exclusively, be the case in arts, humanities and the social sciences.) Whichever is the case, it is important that you leave enough time before the deadline to accommodate such negotiations and to fulfil both the institutional application requirements and those of the funding body.

Different funding bodies have different procedures for reviewing applications for funding for research projects. Only a few use one or more internal reviewers alone to judge the merit of the proposal; instead, many use an internal board or committee made up of research experts from the broad field (but not necessarily people with expertise in a particular discipline area, far less in a specific topic field). The views of this committee may be informed or supplemented by critical reviews from panels of peer researchers. Nevertheless, the vast majority have aspects of the review process in common.

They:

- treat applications in confidence;
- expect reviewers to declare any conflicting interest and withdraw from reviewing applications from their own institution or from colleagues, relatives and others well known to them personally;
- seek unbiased evaluation of the quality of proposals by reviewers, linked to transparent criteria available to the public (usually on websites).

Some funders request outline proposals from which they select a shortlist of applicants who are then requested to provide an extended proposal. Others require the full proposal from which reviewers will select a short list of applicants who may be requested to supply further specific information or to attend an interview (or neither or both). Often the panel will provide a prioritised listing to the board which will then weigh up how many can be funded from available resources. It is frequently the case, in popular discipline areas in particular, that many 'alpha rated' proposals are rejected simply because of insufficient money at the disposal of the board.

Research councils and other large funding organisations do declare their lists of panel members, from which your reviewers will be selected. Such panel members are usually selected to serve for several years, so they are likely to have several, or many, proposals to review. They may also be reviewers for discipline journals as well as the work of their own students. It is wise, therefore, to be considerate when deciding typeface, spacing and other presentational issues because, although they will be trying to be as unprejudiced as possible and attend only to conformity to the published criteria, their patience will naturally be stretched by scripts that are sloppy or difficult to read.

WHAT REVIEWERS ARE SEEKING FROM PROPOSALS

Remember too that funders are accountable, either to the government or to the charities or institutions they represent, so they will expect their reviewers to consider the listed criteria (of which more in a moment) against the backdrop of their mission statements and published target areas. In other words, the quality of the proposals is evaluated against criteria which are fairly standard across the scientific (in its broadest sense) community, while the topic should reflect the current interests, priorities and ambitions laid out on the websites, hence our urging you throughout this text to become thoroughly familiar with this publically available information. Nevertheless, this does not preclude novelty, indeed novelty may form a criterion, but it will be originality that contributes in some important way to the declared purpose and main concerns of the organisation.

Of course, they will also expect proposals to be academically sound, methodologically excellent and feasible, well organised with credible management plans, cost effective and demonstrating clear potential for successful completion with interesting results. Timeliness is another good selling point – a project that addresses an issue that has recently come to attention in some cogent way. In addition, some funders are now keen on projects that include collaboration, across disciplines or institutions, or between the academy and business/industry/the professions.

At the time of writing, a key feature required of proposals in a period of financial austerity is that they demonstrate the potential to have both economic and social impact. This is not the time to be expecting significant funding for research on 'things we do not know much about which might be interesting', although we should not give up hope entirely.

In Box 19 we have collated criteria derived and summarised from multiple sources involved in funding research, in order to give a flavour of what you might find on the website of your favoured funder. If your proposal meets all of these to a very high standard then you are well on your way to success, as long as there is sufficient funding available, of course.

BOX 19 COLLATED CRITERIA FOR JUDGING RESEARCH PROPOSALS

- The rationale is clear, persuasive and detailed.
- It is supported by sound scholarship and evidence from the literature.
- All relevant and significant research in the area has been critically considered.
- It addresses a topic that is current, salient and important.
- The design is coherent and well organised and makes effective use of resources and the time available.
- The approach is appropriate to the research hypothesis/question and consistent.
- The methods and techniques are relevant, described in appropriate detail and are appropriate for the nature and volume of data sought.
- Creative and skilled use is planned for resources/equipment.
- There is evidence of innovation in thought and/or practice.
- Personnel are well qualified for their allotted contributions.
- Administration is well planned.
- Governance issues (ethics, legal issues, permissions and so forth) are sound.
- Appropriate evaluation plans are included.
- There is evidence of support from a well-regarded institution.
- The project budget is well organised and cost-effective.
- References from well-regarded scholars and researchers are enthusiastic and interested in the project.
- The whole proposal demonstrates commitment by the Principal Investigator.
- The research team has a good track record.

- It promises a positive and measurable impact.
- The proposal is culturally sensitive and reflects diversity.
- The results will be disseminated to the academic and professional communities.
- The results will be made available in appropriate forms to potential users.

ACTIVITY 22 REVIEWING YOUR OWN PROPOSAL

This would be a good time to begin an evaluation of your planned inclusions for your proposal as you have produced them so far, judging them using the criteria above. (Of course, if you are applying to engage in a research degree you will be expected to have less experience than those applying for post-doctoral research funding and so will have fewer stringent requirements applied. You will have seen which of these criteria are reduced from reading previous chapters.) Put yourself in the role of a firm but fair reviewer to identify aspects that are missing or could bear improvement.

REALITY CHECK – GRIT YOUR TEETH!

In the Prologue we promised to be realistic and this is the point where we must unpick further just what is meant by our frequent allusions to the process of seeking a place for a *research degree* or *funding for research* being competitive. Earlier we noted that efforts to find a suitable supervisor and be accepted for postgraduate research study have a higher success rate than the rate of positive response to any form of request for financial support. Although we have tried to support your endeavours by encouraging you to put in the best proposal you can, we must at this point be frank and honest by revealing that in both cases, no matter how much effort you make or how polished your bid is, there nevertheless exists a chance that you will receive feedback which indicates either that more work (in the form of revisions) needs to be done or that your proposal has been rejected.

We hasten to assure you that we do not doubt your ability but rather we acknowledge that such results are more common in most disciplines than outright winning of a university place or financial support. In particular, the statistically low success rate for research funding bids is a normal facet of everyday academic life, while having a proposal rejected is one horrible experience that we have all endured, 'we' being academics who strive to continue to do research. But such words do less to help you prepare for all eventualities than the advice we will give you in the next, the last, chapter. Read that before you decide what to do next, but first – pause for thought.

REFLECTION POINT: BUILDING UP YOUR RESILIENCE

This may seem trite, but it is nevertheless true – things that come easily are less valued than those that have to be struggled for, and struggle is defined by there being a good chance of not achieving your aim. Reflect back on your achievements so far, not simply to recognise that you succeeded sometimes against the odds but, more importantly, to identify what sort of things kept you going, provided motivation, when you were knocked back or disappointed in some way. These are resources you might need to draw on again, indeed *will* need to turn to, if you seek an academic career.

10

WHERE DOES IT END? REACTIONS, REFLECTIONS AND ANTICIPATIONS

CHAPTER OVERVIEW

This chapter discusses:

- what to do once the proposal is submitted;
- receiving and responding to feedback;
- possible reasons for rejection;
- a reminder of the importance of refining title, abstract and key words;
- the continuous cycle of proposal writing.

AFTER SUBMISSION

In the first chapter we mentioned the attributes required of researchers as delineated in the Researcher Development Framework (RDF), focussing there on knowledge and cognitive skills. Then in Chapter 3, while discussing plans for the proposed research process, we emphasised the need for perseverance. Now we will add to that list the required attributes of patience and resilience.

Patience will be required because the review process is bound to take time if it is being effectively conducted through the auspices of necessarily busy academics. This patience can be more easily achieved if you keep actively engaged with research-related activities. We will return to that soon. First, we want to pick up the thread from the end of the last chapter about the high probability of rejection, or at least a request for revisions, as we address the need for resilience. We strongly empathise with you in your sense of vulnerability during the period between submission and receiving the response to your proposal. You will have done your best and now you are offering the product up for criticism. It is very much akin to the feelings experienced when you submit your doctoral thesis having crafted it over the course of three to four years of research endeavour.

For each of us the period of waiting for our viva day is etched in memory so much that the stomach butterflies are re-awakened just mentioning it. So for those of you who have submitted a proposal to gain a place on a *research degree* this waiting time is a pilot run for the pre-viva experience. For those requesting *research funding* for a post-doctoral-level project, this period will remind you of that pre-viva time. This may help put this particular wait into proportion – we say this hoping that, although we urge you to give sufficient time to crafting the proposal, you have not taken three to four years' 'full time equivalent' to do so.

Using this period productively not only helps to maintain your patience but also may build up your resilience to any potential disappointment by providing a glimpse of alternative future research activities. Just as you might check your thesis for typographical errors while waiting for the viva in order to show your examiners that you are aware of them, so you might pre-empt the criticism of others and prepare for any suggested revisions by looking for alternative methods for achieving the same aims or at ways of reducing the aims to be more cost effective, and so on. You could also start to think about an alternative institution in case your proposal for a research degree to one does not succeed, or your next potential research project if you are seeking funded research opportunities. We, as experienced academics, have found that having back-up plans B and C and D ready in mind is a useful strategy for most circumstances and certainly assuages some of the inevitable disappointments that come with the territory.

RECEIVING FEEDBACK FROM REVIEWERS

If you receive a positive response from your reviewers then you have every reason to feel elated. It means that the reviewers have fulfilled their job of selecting well-founded, articulated and organised proposals that promise excellent research which also fit the needs and current resources of the organisation they are representing, be it an educational institution or a funding body. In a more sober context it is also their job to provide constructive criticism from that same perspective whether they are suggesting changes to the proposal for a potential re-submission or explaining why they have decided to reject it.

Even though we do recognise that either of the less positive responses will be an initial disappointment, even a shock after you have polished your first submission so carefully, we urge you to re-read the last paragraph very carefully and note that it is the proposal that is being criticised, not you as a person or as a researcher in total, and from a very specific perspective. You might want to wait for a few hours, if not a day or so, from first reading your letter so that you can take in more accurately the detail of what they say once the first shock has passed. Do take heart from the fact that many proposals are rejected that are in themselves excellent, because of a range of reasons not related to inherent defects, as you can see in Box 20. Moreover, the constructive criticism you receive from reviewers will both be informative for this project and help you improve future proposal submissions; we will say more about that later too.

REASONS FOR REJECTION

As we have noted before, not all institutions or funding agencies behave in the same way or have exactly the same criteria for reviewing proposals, so not all will respond with the same amount of detail or suggest or allow re-submissions in the light of revisions using feedback. Some might suggest you revise and re-submit; others will not permit re-submissions. Check this in the organisation's documentation carefully before working on the proposal further. The reasons we have collated in Box 20 assume that you have addressed all the guidance given by the organisation in terms of meeting submission deadlines and adhering to the required structural format.

BOX 20 SOME POSSIBLE REASONS FOR REJECTION

Reasons related to:

- The organisation's remit or structure:
  - Research priorities may have changed since you last read their information source. For an HEI it might be that the appropriate supervisor has left, or has changed research focus; for a funder it might be that government or other stakeholders have new priorities.
  - Research opportunities may have been filled with no spare capacity. For an HEI it might be that the appropriate supervisors have other commitments; for a funder it might be that they have received several excellent proposals in the same area and had to choose only one.

(Continued)

(Continued)

- The organisation's budget:
  - For an HEI it may be that the costs of the project are beyond the means of the department, or the cost outweighs the perceived benefits; for a funder the reasons might be similar or they might judge that the budget was poorly calculated.
- Methods described in the proposal:
  - Both kinds of reviewers might conclude either that the methods are inappropriate for the topic, or are beyond the expertise of the proposer, or are rather too mundane for such an investment.
- The presentation of the proposal:
  - Both kinds of reviewers might decide either that the presentation was incomplete in some way, unclear, careless, biased, or poorly argued or substantiated.

We trust that by the time you have polished your proposal as we have suggested throughout this book the last group of reasons will not apply. We cannot be so sanguine about the penultimate set because choice of methods depends on the epistemology of the reader (see Chapter 6) but at least we expect that you will have justified your choice well. Other aspects of that set of reasons might well form the basis for feedback about changes required for re-submission.

RESPONDING TO FEEDBACK

All of us are vulnerable and get upset when something we have worked hard on does not apparently meet the required standards, but in a system in which far more proposals are received than can be accepted then there will always be some that have to be polished even more to pass the threshold of acceptability whereas others will be rejected totally. Be sure that, whichever category your proposal falls into, you will be in good company. This rigorous selection system has always been an inherent part of the HE system and has become harsher as the economic situation has weakened. So let the initial consternation, sadness, frustration, anger or embarrassment, whichever of these assail you on receipt of a negative letter, fade a little, as they will, before you respond to the reviewers, if that is what is required. You might, of course, simply have to put the letter in your file to act as a source of constructive criticism for guiding your next proposal (which you will have been thinking about while you awaited this result). Alternatively, you might have been invited to re-submit after having reviewed your original submission. (Re-submission requests, like 'minor amendments' following a viva, seem to be becoming more frequent as competition increases and word processing allows for more readily made amendments.)

If this is the case, then calmly review the suggested changes, some of which you might recognise as being genuinely excellent improvements. Others you might be less happy about but remember that suggestions will almost definitely have been made to help your proposal fit better with the requirements of the organisation involved. If they challenge too strongly your dearly held theories and methodological orientation, or if you think that budgetary cuts would seriously restrict your ability to deliver the required product, then you need only politely decline. Do remember that a prompt and polite response is always required if you wish to keep your reputation as a good researcher. By and large most of us find that we can accommodate, and often recognise the value of, the recommendations made. If you find them ambiguous, then telephone or write to the organisation to seek more detail. If you feel that your intentions have been misunderstood, there is no point in a protracted debate; instead, explain them more clearly in the revised version, taking care to reflect the recommendations in your response. You can, in many instances, include a letter in which you indicate what changes you have made in response to each suggested amendment.

What is most important in terms of your response to feedback is that you should take a long view, taking criticism as a contribution to your learning for future efforts, because the nature of the job is that we each make many bids over the course of a research career, only some of which can be successful. Therefore if the proposal, you are considering now is your first, do not let it be your last whatever the outcome. Remember that most of the reasons for rejection are external to your proposal, or your proposal might simply have not caught the attention of the reviewers. Catching and holding attention forms part of the next section, which brings together the components in the proposal-crafting business.

BACK TO THE BEGINNING

When we start writing a proposal most of us design a working title to give ourselves a focus and produce an abstract to give our writing some structure, but often the work then evolves, taking on a life of its own as we:

- work through the theoretical base for the work;
- craft the research questions or hypotheses;
- hone our methodological argument;
- consider the most practical field, desk or laboratory research practice;
- work out the most economic budget;
- debate the most effective dissemination methods.

Before you finally submit your proposal, it is most important to check that your title and abstract still relate to what you have written.

Remember that the title, abstract and key words (if they are required) are what will attract the reviewer in the first place; they are the advertisement, if you like, for the product you wish to sell – your research topic and skills. They need to be accurate in describing the essence of the proposal. Moreover, they need to conform to the length and structure requirements of your target organisation to demonstrate that you know about and respect their criteria. Most importantly, they also need to be stimulating enough to make them stand out in the crowd of other respectful and conforming titles and abstracts.

This final check of these key introductory elements of your document is indispensable, having proof-read the whole document for typographical errors and consistency of terminology, of course. This completes the first turn in the cycle of proposal writing.

THE CONTINUOUS CYCLE OF PROPOSAL WRITING

That last sentence was not a conundrum as you might have thought. Or did you guess that the next turn begins when you have submitted that proposal and begin to contemplate the next research project while you anticipate the response? That new one can either be put aside temporarily if the response is positive or can distract from your chagrin if otherwise. Despite the fact that you know that you will not always be successful, this is the flow of work that contributes to your developing a reputation for effective proposal writing, and this is the only way to ensure a greater success rate.

So put this book down now; there are no more activities or reflection points – you should simply concentrate on actually writing your proposal. In it you might include a commitment to disseminate your results by publishing in a journal. In that case we might meet again in another book in our series that guides readers through the process of writing successful journal articles. Until then, good luck with your research!

Appendix 1

FUNDING SOURCES

RESEARCH COUNCILS IN THE UK FOR STUDENTSHIPS AND RESEARCH GRANTS

Arts and Humanities Research Council (AHRC): www.ahrc.ac.uk
Biotechnology and Biological Sciences Research Council (BBSRC): www.bbsrc.ac.uk
Engineering and Physical Sciences Research Council (EPSRC): www.epsrc.ac.uk
Economic and Social Research Council (ESRC): www.esrc.ac.uk
Medical Research Council (MRC): www.mrc.ac.uk
Natural Environment Research Council (NERC): www.nerc.ac.uk
Science and Technology Facilities Council (STFC): www.STFC.ac.uk

LARGE ACADEMIC CHARITIES OFFERING FULL STUDENTSHIPS

The Wellcome Trust: www.wellcome.ac.uk
The Leverhulme Trust: www.leverhulme.org.uk
The Nuffield Foundation: www.nuffieldfoundation.org
Carnegie Trust: www.carnegie-trust.org

STUDENT FUNDING DATABASES

Scholarship Search: www.scholarship-search.org.uk
Postgraduate Studentships: www.postgraduatestudentships.co.uk

Research and Development Funding (especially 'long shots' section): www.rdfunding.org.uk
Research Professional: www.researchprofessional.com
Student Cash Point: www.studentcashpoint.co.uk

CHARITY SEARCH ENGINES

In the following list, descriptions have been taken from or summarised from the websites.

Charity Commission provides comprehensive information about every registered charity in England and Wales: www.charity-commission.gov.uk
Charity Choice is a comprehensive guide to charities in the UK: www.charitychoice.co.uk
Charities Direct provides alphabetical listings and the top charities tables: www.charitiesdirect.com/charities
Charities Directory includes a free list of charities, non-profit-making organisations, message board, newsletter, sponsors' packages and charity articles: www.charitiesdirectory.com
Charity Portal provides a searchable online database that organises charities by type into logical charity categories and sub-categories: www.charityportal.org.uk
Funder Finder is a small UK charity producing online and offline applications, mainly for grant-seekers based in the UK. Some of the things they produce are free, some cost, though they may be available in libraries: www.funderfinder.org.uk
Guidestar has partner sites in Israel (www.guidestar.org.il), Belgium (www.philanthropy.be) and India (www.guidestarindia.org), and it features a user-friendly search engine to allow free and open access to information on all charities registered in England and Wales: www.guidestar.org.uk
Grantsnet seeks out funders for topics you identify. For example, 'alcohol research' found AERC (Alcohol Education and Research Council: funding alcohol research and development projects as well as providing small grants and studentships to individuals working in the alcohol field.): www.grantsnet.co.uk
Grants Online provides information, including email alerts, on funding from the European Union, UK government, lottery and grant-making trusts: www.grantsonline.org.uk
Turn2us is a free, accessible website that has been designed to help people find appropriate sources of financial support quickly and easily, and has a huge list of potential funders: www.turn2us.org.uk

Some potential funders

Aga Khan Foundation makes grants to students of excellent potential and track record. Usually made to support master's studies (although will consider PhD applicants) and made on a 50 percent grant, 50 percent loan basis. Funds are also available to support travel and research expenses: www.akdn.org/akf_scholarships.asp

Ann Driver Trust provides grants for the study of the arts, especially music, linked to particular institutions: Administrator, Ann Driver Trust, PO Box 2761, London W1A 5HD.

Bernard Butler Trust Fund gives small grants for studying engineering and related disciplines: www.bernardbutlertrust.org/application.php

Cancer Research UK offers a number of full PhD scholarships, obviously in relation to cancer research: www.cancerresearchuk.org

Carnegie Trust awards Carnegie Scholarships to graduates of a Scottish University who hold first-class honours for research in any UK university: www.carnegie-trust.org

Clothworkers' Charity for Education gives small to medium grants for postgraduate students under the age of 25 who live in or are studying in Greater London, or whose parents live in Greater London: www.clothworkers.co.uk

Diabetes UK offers a small number of full PhD scholarships for diabetes research: www.diabetes.org.uk

Leverhulme Trades Charities Trust provides awards for those who can demonstrate a family link (i.e. parents or spouse) with the grocers' trade, chemists or pharmacists, or commercial travellers: www.leverhulme-trade.org.uk

McGlashan Charitable Trust takes applicants for grants from those either studying or working in Scotland, or those who have been born in Scotland: PO Box 16057, Glasgow G12 9XX.

Noon Foundation gives educational grants to students from Pakistan: The Trustees, 25 Queen Anne's Gate St. James Park, London SW1H 9BU. Email: secretary@noongroup.co.uk

Royal Bath and West of England Society offers grants for any aspect of agriculture, horticulture, forestry, conservation or any form of food production or marketing: Jane Guise, The Showground, Shepton Mallet, Somerset BA4 6QN.

Royal Geographical Society makes awards for research expenses and travel for the study of geography: www.rgs.org

Wingate Foundation gives scholarships to students in the final year of their course, based on record and financial need (with a preference for inter-disciplinary studies): www.wingatescholarships.org.uk

FUNDING GUIDE SITES

Educational Grants Advisory Service: www.family-action.org/section
Prospects Student Funding Guides: www.prospects.ac.uk/funding_my_further_study.htm
Turn2us Guide on Grants and Funding: www.turn2us.org.uk/information_resources.aspx
Unigrants: www.unigrants.co.uk

Raising funds in North America

Big Online is a comprehensive source of fundraising information, opportunities and resources for charities and non-profits: www.bigdatabase.com
Forum of Regional Associations of Grantmakers is a national philanthropic leader and a network of thirty-two regional associations of Grantmakers: www.givingforum.org
Foundation Search America is an online resource including more than 120,000 foundations and tools to locate grants by type, value, year, etc.: www.foundationsearch.com
Grantsearch is a database designed for Grants Resource Center institutions (members of the American Association of State Colleges and Universities), and profiles more than 2000 federal and private funding programmes that focus on higher education: www.aascu.org

Raising funds in Europe

European Foundation Centre is an international, not-for-profit association promoting and supporting the work of active European foundations: www.efc.be
Funders Online is a source of information on foundations and corporate funders active in Europe; also provides links to Europe's online philanthropic community. Remember to click on the 'translate' button if you do not speak German: www.fundersonline.org

Raising funds in international contexts

Women's Funding Network is an international organisation with over 100 member funds that are committed to improving the status of women and girls: www.wfnet.org

DIRECTORIES AND BOOKS

The Alternative Guide to Postgraduate Funding (2011) by Luke Blaxill and Shuzhi Zhou. London: Grad Funding.

Provides the tools and guidance needed to access charitable funding, a major but neglected source of postgraduate financial support.

Charities Digest (annual). London: Waterlow Professional Publishing.

A handbook for those seeking help, providing advice services or referencing information on charities.

The Guide to Educational Grants 2011/12 (2011) by S. Johnston. London: Directory of Social Change (DSC).

A comprehensive listing of national and local charities which give to individuals for education. Published every two years.

The Grants Register. Basingstoke: Palgrave Macmillan.

The most comprehensive guide available to postgraduate grants and professional funding worldwide. For 28 years the leading source for up-to-date information on the availability of, and eligibility for, postgraduate and professional awards. All information is updated annually.

Appendix 2

RESOURCES

BOOKS ON PROPOSAL CONSTRUCTION AND/OR GRANT APPLICATIONS

The following books have guided the learning of the authors over their years of working in the field of research or have been particularly recommended by colleagues from across the wide context of global research.

UK-orientated books

Berry, D.C. (2010) *Gaining Funding for Research: A Guide for Academics and Institutions*. Maidenhead: Open University Press.

A detailed discussion about the implications of research for academic careers and for academic institutions, this book reviews the main forms of research and sources of funding in the UK and how to improve chances of gaining funding. This is a very useful book for more experienced researchers with some experience in the system. It does have extensive appendices which contain, inter alia, the assessment criteria of the main funding councils and some examples of well-worded proposal sections.

Day, P.A. (2003) *Winning Research Funding*. Aldershot: Gower.

In contrast to the previous book, this one is more discursive in style, with short, pithy sections on each step of the process, interspersed with extensive quotations from documents and practitioners in the field: researchers and reviewers. The focus is on identifying funding partners and building a strong relationship with them, and might appeal most to a novice researcher.

Books from other national contexts

Carlson, M. and O'Neal-McElrath, T. (2008) *Winning Grants: Step by Step*. San Francisco, CA: Jossey-Bass.

A very practical guide, with numerous worksheets, focussed on raising funding in the US context.

Coley, S.M. and Scheinberg, C.A. (2008) *Proposal Writing: Effective Grantsmanship*. Thousand Oaks, CA: SAGE.

A simple, jargon-free guide to obtaining grants for research programmes and for supporting research students in the US context.

Locke, L.F., Spirduso, W.W. and Silverman, S.J. (2007) *Proposals that Work: A Guide for Planning Dissertations and Grant Proposals*. Thousand Oaks, CA: SAGE.

This book covers succinctly the whole process of proposal writing within the US context with practical advice, and examples and samples of experimental and interpretative studies and an annotated bibliography. This is more helpful for those with at least a beginning familiarity with the jargon of US Higher Education than for novices.

Ogden, T.E. and Goldberg, I.A. (1991) *Research Proposals: A Guide to Success*. San Diego, CA: Elsevier/Academic Press.

This is a 'how to' guide that has a particular emphasis on writing proposals to the US National Institutes of Health. It includes extensive appendices which provide information sources, design formats, instructions to reviewers and examples of reviewers' comments, amongst other useful information.

Punch, K.F. (2000) *Developing Effective Research Proposals*. London: SAGE.

Although the main focus of this book is on proposals for gaining funding for research degrees and therefore places much emphasis on research design and methods, it provides two examples of proposals from the Australian context and notes other examples to be found in the literature.

Ward, D. (2006) *Writing Grant Proposals that Win*. Boston, MA: Jones and Bartlett.

Again, this is a step-by-step guide derived from the US context. It usefully provides details of five successful proposals in that context.

BOOKS FOR THOSE CONTEMPLATING EMBARKING ON A RESEARCH DEGREE

Hall, G. and Longman, J. (eds) (2008) *The Postgraduate's Companion*. London: SAGE.

Wellington, J. (2010) *Making Supervision Work for You: A Student's Guide*. London: SAGE.

RESEARCH METHODS BOOKS – GENERAL

Gray, D.E. (2009) *Doing Research in the Real World*. London: SAGE.

Kumar, R. (2011) *Research Methodology: A Step by Step Guide for Beginners*. London: SAGE.

Locke, L., Silverman, S.J. and Spirduso, W.W. (2004) *Reading and Understanding Research*. Thousand Oaks, CA: SAGE.

Rumsey, S. (2008) *How to Find Information: A Guide for Researchers*. Maidenhead: Open University Press.

AN INDICATIVE LIST OF RESEARCH METHODS BOOKS FOR DIFFERENT DISCIPLINES

This list is intended to demonstrate the range of books available that focus on the practice of research as it occurs in different disciplines. They each draw on generic research methods but provide information on approaches and techniques that are common in or favoured by the particular discipline.

Ackerson, L.G. (ed.) (2007) *Literature Search Strategies for Interdisciplinary Research: A Sourcebook for Scientists and Engineers*. Lanham, MD: Scarecrow Press.

Adams, L.S. (1996) *The Methodologies of Art: An Introduction*. New York: IconEditions.

Clifford, N. and Valentine, G. (eds) (2003) *Key Methods in Geography*. London: SAGE.

Cohen, J. and Medley, G. (2000) *Stop Working and Start Thinking: A Guide to Becoming a Scientist*. Cheltenham: Stanley Thornes.

Cohen, L., Manion, L. and Morrison, K. (2011) *Research Methods in Education*. Abingdon: Routledge.

Daymon, C. and Holloway, I. (2010) *Qualitative Research in Public Relations and Marketing Communications*. Abingdon: Routledge.

Fellows, R.F. and Liu, A. (2008) *Research Methods for Construction*. Chichester: Wiley-Blackwell.

Flowerdew, R. and Martin, D. (eds) (1997) *Methods in Human Geography: A Guide for Students Doing a Research Project*. Harlow: Pearson-Prentice Hall.

Harner, J.L. (2002) *Literary Research Guide: An Annotated Listing of Reference Sources in English Literature Studies*. New York: Modern Languages Association of America.

Holmes, D., Moody, P. and Dine, D. (2006) *Research Methods for the Biosciences*. Oxford: Oxford University Press.

McDowell, W.H. (2002) *Historical Research: A Guide*. London: Longman.

RESOURCES RELATED TO PROPOSAL WRITING AND SPECIFIC SECTIONS OF THE PROPOSAL

Aveyard, H. (2007) *Doing a Literature Review in Health and Social Care – A Practical Guide*. Maidenhead: Open University Press.

A user-friendly beginners' guide to different forms of review and how and why they are used, with great detail about many topics touched on in preceding chapters of this book (e.g. developing a systematic approach, critical appraisal and selection of literature, synthesising findings, examples from qualitative and quantitative studies).

Crème, P. and Lea, M.R. (1997) *Writing at University*. Maidenhead: Open University Press.

What writing is for: methods and approaches to gain control over academic writing – for those new to or distant from academic style or English conventions.

Dey, I. (1993) *Qualitative Data Analysis: A User Friendly Guide for Social Scientists*. Abingdon: Routledge.

Learning how to analyse qualitative data by computer can be fun! This book contains examples drawn from everyday life and is suitable for a wide audience.

EndNote website: www.endnote.com/support

Provides technical support, and updates to filter, as well as connection and output style files. Useful FAQs and tip sheets. There is an international forum for EndNote users to ask questions, make suggestions and get advice on any EndNote-related topic – however basic or advanced. You can search the website to find archives of old discussions: http://community.thomsonreuters.com/ (accessed August 2011).

Evans, D. and Gruba, P. (2002) *How to Write a Better Thesis*. Victoria, Australia: Melbourne University Press.

Emphasis on clear and logical structure with concrete examples and practical suggestions. A full chapter is given to making use of computer software to aid thesis production for presentation, creating and using a template, and document management.

Fink, A. (2005) *Conducting Research Literature Reviews: From the Internet to Paper*. London: SAGE.

A more advanced text with a particularly useful section on key words, doing searches online and different kinds of literature reviews.

Neville, C. (2007) *The Complete Guide to Referencing and Avoiding Plagiarism*. Maidenhead: Open University Press.

The book gives guidance on how to cite external sources correctly, what constitutes plagiarism and how it can be avoided. It contains a useful FAQs section – including information on referencing electronic sources.

Oliver, P. (2003) *The Student's Guide to Research Ethics*. Maidenhead: Open University Press.

This book provides examples and case studies for both beginners and more experienced researchers to help them to identify ethical issues and attempt to resolve them.

Rugg, G. (2007) *Using Statistics: A Gentle Introduction*. Maidenhead: Open University Press.

With an informal, entertaining style, this book covers the range from simple descriptive to multidimensional approaches, with numerous illustrations from a broad discipline base.

Rumsey, S. (2008) *How to Find Information: A Guide for Researchers*. Maidenhead: Open University Press.

This book enables researchers to become experts in finding, accessing and evaluating information for projects or reports; this edition is updated to include use of new technologies.

Sinclair, C. (2007) *Grammar: A Friendly Approach*. Maidenhead: Open University Press.

This is a grammar book with a difference. It brings grammar to life with examples of grammatical problems, and examines and clearly explains language use, such as active and passive voice, and punctuation, such as colons, semi-colons and apostrophes.

Thomson, P. and Walker, M. (eds) (2010) *The Routledge Doctoral Student's Companion: Getting to Grips with Research in Education and the Social Sciences*. Abingdon: Routledge.

This is a comprehensive and accessible guide to the literature (particularly focussing on what doctoral education means), becoming a researcher and the skills needed to conduct research.

Wallace, M. and Wray, A. (2006) *Critical Reading and Writing for Postgraduates*. London: SAGE.

A step-by-step guide to critically reading others' and your own writing, evaluating authors' arguments, building your own arguments and integrating critical reviews into a thesis.

GLOSSARY

Action research Research undertaken as a partnership between the researcher and the practitioners (of whom the researcher might be one) in their context that is focussed on a practical problem the resolution of which will benefit the context and those in it.

Aim The intent of the research, couched at a general level.

Audit trail The research material produced by interpretivist enquiry presented to demonstrate a clear and transparent link between the raw data, analysed data and conclusions.

Audit record (finance) The organised collection of invoices and receipts related to a project's costs.

Authenticity The extent to which participants in interpretive research would recognise the resulting data as representing their world.

Case study A research design focussing on one person, situation or organisation which traditionally involves in-depth study using a range of techniques or one or more techniques over a lengthy time period to produce detailed information.

Co-investigator A person who assists the grant holder in the management and leadership of a project.

Conceptual framework The central concepts of a research project organised to illustrate their relationship to one another. It can be presented as a diagram.

Confidence level A statistical measure of the extent that results obtained are significant or likely to be true, usually given as a percentage.

Confirmability The degree to which comparable results could be obtained by another researcher following the same research process.

Confounding variable A variable, other than the dependent and independent variables, which might distort the results of experimental research, and so must be controlled.

Construct An expression of an individual's perception/understanding of the meaning about a concept.

Constructivism A perspective that assumes that people construe the realities in which they participate in an individual way, constructing meaning from that construal.

Control group A group *not* subject to an experimental intervention that provides data with which to contrast the results from the experimental group.

Correlation The relationship between and among interdependent variables such that when one variable changes, so does the other. Variables that are independent are not correlated.

Credibility The degree to which participants would judge the research results to represent their perspectives in interpretive research.

Curation (of data) Selection, organisation and care of information gained through an investigation.

Data Findings and results which, if meaningful, become information.

Deductive approach Experimental approach that uses a-priori questions or hypotheses that the research will test.

Dependability Degree to which the data are recognised over time by participants as relating to their world.

Dependent variable A variable that is assumed by the hypothesis to depend for its value on the changes in another (the independent) variable.

Descriptive statistics Statistical methods used to describe data collected from a specific sample (e.g. frequencies, dimensions).

Design The structured approach to the collection of data that seeks to provide valid or authentic results using the most appropriate instruments in the most efficient and productive way.

Directly allocated costs The costs of resources used by a project that are shared with other activities. They are charged to the projects on the basis of estimates rather than actual costs. (These might be a share of the running costs of equipment or for goods bought in bulk for use across projects, for instance.)

Directly incurred costs Costs that are explicitly identifiable as arising from the conduct of the project, are charged as the cash value actually spent and are supported by an audit record (i.e. invoices and receipts of transactions are available).

Discourse analysis The study of the structure and content of language, written or spoken.

Empirical data The results of research techniques used to check the validity/authenticity of assertions and assumptions.

Epistemology The theory of knowledge and how it is acquired.

Ethics The study of codes and principles of moral behaviour, and in research, decisions about which courses of action are morally right or wrong, particularly in terms of their impact on participants/subjects and the communities they belong to.

Ethnography An interpretive approach that researches the perspectives and the culture of individuals, groups or systems occurring in settings or 'fields'.

Ethnomethodology A research tradition that argues that people continually redefine themselves through their interactions with others.

Evaluation An assessment or evaluation of the worth of a phenomenon and the systematic collection of data about it.

Experiment A predominantly positivist research design in which variables are manipulated or controlled to observe the effect on other variables, or in which research subjects are randomly assigned to experimental or control conditions and the results on a predetermined test observed.

Experimental group In experimental research, the group of subjects who receive the experimental treatment, in contrast to the control group who do not.

Full economic cost (fEC) A cost which, if recovered across an organisation's full programme, would recover the total cost (direct, indirect and total overhead) including an adequate recurring investment in the organisation's infrastructure.

Full economic costing A policy to support the UK government's requirements to improve the sustainability of research and other HE activities by recovering as much as possible of the full costs from research sponsors, thus reducing the drain on resources supplied through central funding of universities.

Full-time equivalent (fte) A figure representing a proportion as it would be applicable to a full-time student or member of academic staff. For instance: a part-time student may be 0.5 fte in terms of expected effort; a staff member might contribute one day per week to a project, which would be 0.2 fte.

Generalizable results Those research results that though obtained from a sample can justifiably be extended to apply to the whole population.

Grant Support for a proportion of the full economic cost of a project.

Grant holder The person to whom the grant is assigned and who has responsibility for the intellectual leadership of the project and for the overall management of the research. In the case of a research grant this is the Principal Investigator (PI).

Grounded theory A research approach that begins by making no assumptions in advance based on literature/previous research. Theory is built up by induction using the analysed results of the empirical work.

Hermeneutics An approach based on the interpretation of literary texts and human behaviour in terms of the socio-cultural meanings brought to them by the writers.

Hypothesis A statement that should be capable of measurement about the relation between two or more variables. Testing hypotheses, and especially the null hypothesis, is part of inferential statistics.

Ideographic Related to the study of individuals or small cases in a holistic, naturalistic way despite their inherent complexity in order to gain an understanding of them.

Independent variable Used to explain or predict a result or outcome on the dependent variable.

Indirect costs Non-specific costs charged across all projects based on estimates that are not otherwise included as Directly Allocated Costs. They include the costs of the Research Organisation's administration such as personnel, finance, library and some departmental services (such as IT).

Induction The development of theory or inferences from observed or empirical reality. It is associated with naturalism and the 'grounded theory' approach to theory formation. It is the opposite of deduction.

Inferential statistics Tests used to determine the probability that the results of research are the result of the research conditions or to chance alone.

Informed consent Voluntary agreement to take part in a research project based on a full understanding of the likely benefits and risks.

Instrument A tool such as a questionnaire, survey or observation schedule used to gather data as part of a research project.

Interpretivism The philosophical approaches that contend that we have no way of directly knowing reality so instead adopt a more adaptive and active view of knowledge as interpretations of the world. These approaches include constructivism, phenomenology, ethnomethodology, hermeneutics and naturalistic enquiry.

Interview The seeking of views in verbal form, either in person or by telephone or video conference, from respondents. The interview might be very structured with pre-formed and organised questions, less structured (semi-structured) with topics and general questions formulated in advance, or very unstructured with only the general topic area identified and very open-ended questions or trigger questions used. The data from the first variety are likely to be analysed in a quantitative way whereas analysis becomes increasingly qualitative for the remaining two varieties.

Iterative design An approach in which the results of one cycle in the process informs the next, and the results of successive cycles are used to refine the ideas generated in earlier cycles.

Literature review A critical evaluation of the most relevant documents (published and unpublished) on an issue in relation to a particular piece of research.

Manipulation Intentionally changing the value of the independent variable.

Methodology The theoretical and philosophical case for the choice of research approach, design and techniques, including data analysis techniques as well as data collection tools.

Mixed-method research Empirical research that draws on both qualitative and quantitative data to explore and understand a research topic.

Narratives The use of oral or life histories to capture personal lived experiences.

Nomothetic Approaches that seek to generate scientific laws that explain and predict behaviour.

Null hypothesis (*H0*) A statement that no relationship exists between two variables. When the null hypothesis is rejected at a statistically significant level then it is considered that the hypothesised relationship does exist.

Objective methods Methods intended to be free from bias.

Objectives Specific outputs sought by the implementation of the project that contribute to achieving the aim of the project.

Observation A set of techniques using the senses to collect data, ranging, like interviews, from very structured approaches yielding quantitative data to more open approaches providing qualitative data about what actions are perceived to be taking place in naturalist or defined settings and who is involved in them.

Ontology The study of the essence of phenomena and the nature of their existence.

Open questions These questions seek to allow the respondents the widest possible choice about how to answer them, not guiding them in any way other than to consider the general topic. This minimises researcher bias.

Overheads Expenses incurred in running premises, such as building maintenance, heating, lighting and furnishing, and taxes and/or in employing persons, such as employers' National Insurance and pension contributions.

Paradigm A basic set of beliefs, values and assumptions that guide action and include the researcher's epistemological, ontological and methodological premises.

Participants Those people who take part in research of an interpretivist/constructivist nature and provide data for the research. They might also include the researcher, for example, in action research.

Phenomenology This approach deals with how people experience objects, phenomena and events in the world and what meaning they have for them.

Population The people, organisations, objects or occurrences from which a sample is drawn.

Positivism A philosophical assumption that the world exists outside the knower, that knowledge comes from collecting empirical observations and that we can develop coherent systems of knowledge (theories) through testing of hypotheses and logical deduction.

Post-test A test that occurs after an intervention has taken place in an experimental study.

Pre-test A test that occurs before an intervention has taken place in an experimental study.

Qualitative methods Techniques by which qualitative data are collected and analysed.

Quantitative methods The systematic and mathematical techniques used to collect and analyse quantitative data.

Quasi-experimental design A design that uses attributes or elements of experimental and non-experimental design when only some of the parameters of an experimental design can be obtained.

Random sample A sample of the whole population in which each element has an equal chance of being selected – the choice of one element is not dependent in any way on the choice of another.

Reductionist This describes research that pares the number of variables down to the minimum possible in order to study the effect of one variable on another/others without contamination of other factors that may occur at the same time, thus reducing the complexity of the situation. This contrasts with holist research that seeks to study phenomena in the complex situation in which they normally occur.

Reflexivity The monitoring by a researcher of her or his impact on the research situation being investigated, often through the use of a reflective log that becomes part of the research data. This stance is associated with interpretive approaches and postmodernism.

Reliability The degree to which an instrument will produce similar results regardless of whoever uses it or whenever it is used.

Repertory grid One of several tools from personal construct psychology devised both to elicit in a more or less structured way (depending on form chosen) the ways in which individuals construe objects, people or events, and to present the data in a form that allows for relationships between constructs to be mapped.

Representative sample A sample which mirrors the nature of the whole population in terms of proportions of individual types.

Research design A strategic, procedural plan for a research project, setting out the broad structures and features of the research, each with justification.

Research grant A contribution to the costs of a stated research project which has been assessed as suitable for funding through the procedures established by the relevant funding body.

Research organisation The organisation to which the grant is awarded and which takes responsibility for the management of the project and the accountability of funds provided. (That is why it is critically important to engage an HEI's Research Accounting Team in the bidding process – not only for the help they can provide but also to respect their accountability.)

Research question A specific formulation of the objectives of the research project, often querying the general relationships between phenomena or the meanings attributed to them.

Sample A sub-group of a population chosen for research when the total population is too large to study.

Significance level The probability of rejecting a true null hypothesis. This should be chosen before a test is performed and should be low enough to prevent the null hypothesis being rejected when it is in fact true.

Statistically significant Using inferential statistics to conclude that a particular result is very unlikely to have occurred by chance; such a result is therefore accepted as being the result of the research intervention.

Subjects A term most frequently used in positivist research to describe those who participate in a research study.

Survey The collection of information from a sample of a population, using a questionnaire that might elicit both qualitative and quantitative date.

Thick description A detailed account of life 'inside' a field of study.

Transferability The degree to which the results of naturalistic or interpretive research can be transferred to other contexts or groups.

Transparent Approach to Costing (TRAC) An agreed methodology used by universities and other HE bodies for calculating full economic costs.

Triangulation A design that involves two or more methods or techniques for collecting data on a topic, providing both additional data and an opportunity to compare perspectives and either substantiate or modify alternative interpretations.

Unstructured interview This kind of interview allows respondents to follow their own thread through the interview with the provision only of the general topic and encouragement to elaborate. This allows the researcher to note the concerns and interests of the interviewee, uncontaminated by the researcher's own opinions and understandings.

Utility This is the extent to which data serves a useful purpose to those who provide it, collect it or may have some other stake in knowing about it.

Validity The ability of an instrument to measure what it is designed to measure, that is, the degree to which resultant data are appropriate, accurate and credible.

Value judgements Moral or ethical judgements; judgements of what is good or bad, right or wrong, etc.

Variable A concept that can take on different values and that is measurable.

REFERENCES

Hofstadter, D.R. (1985) *Metamagical Themas: Questing for the Essence of Mind and Pattern*. Harmondsworth: Penguin.

Research Councils UK (RCUK) (2011) 'What do research councils mean by impact?' Accessed February 2011: www.rcuk.ac.uk/kei/impact/Pages/meanbyimpact.aspx

Vitae (2011) 'Researcher development statement and researcher development framework'. Accessed May 2011: www.vitae.ac.uk/policy-practice/Researcher-Development-Framework/RDF

INDEX